# A Mad Love
### and
# A Shameless Audacity

"In *A Mad Love and a Shameless Audacity*, Brandon Ryan gets personal about his journey with the grace of God. Battling through the challenges of cerebral palsy and the discouragement of friends seeming to lose their faith along the way, Brandon doubles down on a hunger to know Christ more, and to accept the acceptance that belongs to him as a son of God. Shameless audacity – the courage to be himself and to press onward in life – comes from receiving the mad love with which God loves him in Christ. Befitting his martial arts background, Brandon Ryan writes like a grappler. He wrestles between self-criticism and self-acceptance, between God's grace and human choices to flee from grace. This is not a book that ties up all loose ends. This is a transparent book that gets into issues that don't necessarily get talked about when Christian men get together. But they are real and the places where God's grace means the most. *A Mad Love and a Shameless Audacity* brings a message of encouragement for readers who feel alone in their struggles, and a bracing challenge for those who are willing to believe in Christ as Savior: to accept that our identity in Christ – not the picture we've had of ourselves in the past – is who we truly are now."
**Andrew "Roo" Burnett, PhD**. Pastor

"Brandon Ryan reminds us that we, as Christians, are always learning to walk with the Lord who loves us so deeply. *A Mad Love and a Shameless Audacity* is a straight-forward guide full of important information for those of us who want to enjoy the companionship of our Lord and to allow God to love us and let His love move over the old scars and pains in our lives. This is a must-read for anyone who is searching for truth or wondering if the Lord hears and cares and understands."
**Cathy Martin, PhD**. Christian Counselor

"With raw honesty, Brandon shares his journey with Jesus. Brandon takes you through his story in a way that you feel what he's been through – as if it was your story and not his. He wraps it all together in a way that you sense the mad love and shameless audacity of the Lord he follows, the love of Jesus. Brandon's story is a great one for someone who needs motivation to keep walking through difficult things!"
**Ryan Pramberg**. Youth Pastor

# A Mad Love

and

# A Shameless Audacity

BRANDON RYAN

*A Mad Love and Shameless Audacity*
Copyright © 2021 by Brandon Ryan

All rights reserved. No part of this publication may be reproduced, stored in a retrieval system, or transmitted in any form or by any means—electronic, mechanical, photocopy, recording, or any other—except for brief quotations in printed reviews, without the prior permission of the publisher.

Scripture quotations marked (ESV) are from The ESV® Bible (The Holy Bible, English Standard Version®), copyright © 2001 by Crossway, a publishing ministry of Good News Publishers. Used by permission. All rights reserved.

Scripture quotations marked (NIV) are taken from the Holy Bible, New International Version®, NIV®. Copyright © 1973, 1978, 1984, 2011 by Biblica, Inc.™ Used by permission of Zondervan. All rights reserved worldwide. www.zondervan.com. The "NIV" and "New International Version" are trademarks registered in the United States Patent and Trademark Office by Biblica, Inc.™

Scripture marked (NKJV) taken from the New King James Version®. Copyright © 1982 by Thomas Nelson. Used by permission. All rights reserved.

McGAHAN PUBLISHING HOUSE
www.mphbooks.com
Requests for information should be sent to:
info@mphbooks.com

Cover Design by Andrew Waters

ISBN 978-1-951252-08-3

# Contents

Preface: Thoughts Moving Forward ........................ vii
Returning to the Heart .................................... 13
Seeing God Is Seeing Love ................................ 19
Letting Abba Ignite the Spark ............................ 23
Accept the Acceptance .................................... 32
When Jesus Enters Your Home ............................ 37
He Delights ................................................ 41
The Old Man .............................................. 47
His Great Pleasure ........................................ 53
When We Fade ............................................ 56
Becoming Less ............................................ 60
His Love Compels Us to Move ............................ 62
My Unfaithfulness and His Faithfulness ................. 68
My Greatest Reward ...................................... 73
You Were Such a … ....................................... 80
A Constant Smile ......................................... 86
A Divine Trust ............................................ 91
Light ...................................................... 97
The Spiritual Glue ....................................... 101

| | |
|---|---|
| Awaiting the New You | 105 |
| The Heavy Soul | 110 |
| For the Sensitive Soul | 114 |
| Silencing the Enemy | 120 |
| The God Who Haunts | 128 |
| Anger | 138 |
| The Sudden Longing | 145 |
| His Grace | 156 |
| For the Outcast | 162 |
| Seeing the Glory | 170 |
| A Mad Love Legacy | 178 |

# PREFACE
# Thoughts Moving Forward

I HAVEN'T WRITTEN anything in months, at least not anything that I would consider worthy of publication. I'm lucky to be typing away on a laptop; if it was on pen and paper, I probably would have killed hundreds of trees by now. I would start typing something and delete it moments later because I didn't see any value or worth in what I was writing. I would start writing on a topic and think to myself, "Wait, somebody else already wrote on that, and it's probably a lot better." Or, even worse, "Nobody cares about that topic." There was a huge longing inside for what Stephen King had, the fact that when he would crumple up his writings and toss them in the trash, he had a wife who would go and get his writing from the trash, un-crumple it, and tell him it wasn't garbage.

I wanted the same thing in my life, and when I didn't get what I wanted, my heart began to despair. There were many times where I looked down into my hands and said, "God, I'm not sure I can do this. I don't think I'll ever make decent money or be a New York Times bestseller. Maybe I should stick with something else that I'm actually good at." But, after some time had passed, I began to think that maybe God didn't care whether or not I made millions of dollars or was a New York Times bestseller. Maybe He simply cared that I was telling people about Him. Part of the problem, I'll admit, was not that I was writing the same thing over and over, but that I was writing about God all over again.

Was I ashamed of God? I don't know for sure, but for the sake of transparency, I'll admit that might have been part of the issue in order to give more context to what was going on in my life over the past handful of years. In summary, I have had a handful of close friends state that they could no longer accept the orthodox teachings of the Christian faith. This encompassed the Bible and all the big things concerning Jesus Christ. Each time this would happen, it felt as though a knife was being driven into my chest. I thought I was losing some of my closest friends. There was a time in my faith journey where I could go back and forth when people argued about the Bible and the existence of God, but when it came to my closest friends, everything in my mind and body seemed to shut down. Was there something inside me that stopped loving my friends? Heavens, no! The truth of the matter is, I collapsed under the arguments against the faith that I had.

I felt like a horrible evangelist and Christian apologist (someone who gives an answer for the faith they have). So, instead of being strong and full of courage, I ran away like a coward. I loved Jesus and deeply believed in what He had done for me on the cross, as well as His defeat of death, but I was also frustrated with the fact that I could not give a good enough rebuttal to any of my friends. Furthermore, I was frustrated because it seemed like God wasn't doing anything. Part of me also didn't trust God, so my worrying and fretting became something I devoted much of my time to. What could I say to make others come to the saving knowledge of Christ? What could I do to make Christ look more attractive? To answer the first question, the best thing I knew how to do was pray. When it came to my friends turning away from Christ, the grief was too much and came with a host of other emotions such as love, passion, anger, and frustration.

As it relates to the second question, I'm not sure there was anything I could have done to make Christ more appealing or attractive. Even simply loving others can sometimes be taken as being a good moral person without any sort of higher law beyond it. The cliché phrase, "let go and let God," comes to mind at this moment, but I don't see it as completely giving up. Rather, I will fight for my friends and loved ones in ways that cannot be seen by human eyes. Jesus tells us that when we pray, we should pray behind closed doors (Matthew 6:5-6). That tends to be what happens. More often than not, my head will hit the pillow, and I'll pray while falling asleep or later in the shower. I never wanted to cause a spectacle by praying for a friend in public. I'm not opposed to it; I just know how creepy it can sometimes be. I was with some people at a movie theater once, and as we were walking into our selected theater, a couple stopped me and asked if they could pray for me. I automatically said no. It wasn't that I was opposed to prayer, but I had an odd feeling that things might get a little out of hand, especially in a public setting. I knew they would probably lay hands on me, which is fine, but I wanted to prevent them from having the opportunity of breaking out in tongues (prayer language). Again, it isn't that I'm opposed to prayer, especially in a public setting. It's that I didn't want a crazy Baptist or Charismatic scene unfolding to create a show, rather than to bring honor to God.

I can remember a close friend of mine with whom I was sitting at our college dining hall, and he looked at me and said, "I know of God, but I don't know God." As I looked into his eyes, I saw tears beginning to develop. I think I remember saying something to the effect of, "It'll be okay," as I put my hand on his arm. I remember mostly listening to what he had to say with great intent, and, at the end of our meal together, I remember asking him if I could pray for him. As he agreed, I prayed with compassion and earnest desire for him to know Christ as I did. a

Since that moment, my friend has gone on a long quest, discovering what various fields of science have to say about how the world was made and how humans are. He has also read a number of popular atheists' writings about why they detest Christianity altogether. Ultimately, he found no reason to believe that the Bible is the Word of God or that it was divinely inspired. Furthermore, he understood that evolution makes far more sense than believing in creation. Again, I had no answers for him. In fact, I had no answers for much of what was going on at this point in my life. I felt like I was losing one of my best friends. In all honestly, it felt as though my grief was centered around the death of a family member. To this day, I still blame myself for not saying more at the dinner table with him. I even blame myself for not having more of a rebuttal toward his arguments against the faith that I had. I wish I understood science and apologetics better, and nothing says that I can't. But, many times, it all seems way over my head.

Even when I took apologetics during my junior year of college, I probably only understood about five percent of what was taught. Maybe it was all my fault, or perhaps it was partly the teacher's fault; I'm not sure. All I know is that a lot of my classmates struggled, too. The fact is, I still feel bad for not taking more with me, for not being able to accurately provide Christian explanations for how the world was made. But, in all of the doubts concerning my own abilities as a Christian, I realized, one, that I am not God, and, two, that people make their own choices in life. The hard truth of the matter is, sometimes you have to move on. I've come to realize that I am not the guy to have a three-hour debate with someone. I don't mind listening to people; hence I'm a psychology major. But there comes the point at which you have to let people live in their choices. In the book of Matthew (10:13-15), Jesus speaks these words to his disciples:

"And if the house is worthy, let your peace come upon it, but if it is not worthy, let your peace return to you. And if anyone will not receive you or listen to your words, shake off the dust from your feet when you leave that house or town. Truly, I say to you, it will be more bearable on the day of judgment for the land of Sodom and Gomorrah than for that town" (ESV). Scripture tells us that we should always be willing to give an answer for the hope that we have (1 Peter 3:15), and Christians love keeping this verse ready at all times. To be honest, though, I have felt burdened by this verse. The reason is that I don't want to engage with a hardened atheist who is only looking to verbally assault me as a Christian, though I'm not shocked by it—it's to be expected. When it came to big-named atheists, I never ever wanted to get into a yelling match with them; it never seemed fruitful to me, and in the end, it would only leave me drained as a sensitive person. More than anything in my life right now, I see myself as a praying man who is hungry to know Christ. I guess you could say I'm rekindling the fire for my faith (I never left), but I miss the old me, and as much as I can't go back in time, I can still carry the flame moving forward.

**Brandon Lee Ryan**

"Do you believe that the God of Jesus loves you beyond worthiness and unworthiness, beyond fidelity and infidelity—that he loves you in the morning sun and in the evening rain—that he loves you when your intellect denies it, your emotions refuse it, your whole being rejects it? Do you believe that God loves without condition or reservation and loves you this moment as you are and not as you should be?"

- Brennan Manning

*All is Grace: A Ragamuffin Memoir*

# 1
# Returning to the Heart

> "For God so loved the world, that he gave his only Son, that whoever believes in him should not perish but have eternal life."
> John 3:16 (ESV)

THE WORLD SEEMS to be spinning out of control. Violence seems to have the upper hand, and, more than ever, it seems that believing in God is more or less something to be laughed at. From my vantage point, it seems like Christianity, at least the American variety, is rapidly dissolving from the inside out. At the Bible college I attend, we are very scattered in our various theological stances and opinions, which isn't always a bad thing. However, it can become a very bad thing when we spend a lot of time talking about others with whom we don't agree or those who do not agree with us. It becomes a problem when we as believers backbite on one another and tear each other down rather than building up. Scripture tells us (through the Apostle Paul) in 2 Corinthians 13:9-11, "We are glad whenever we are weak, but you are strong; and our prayer is that you may be fully restored. This is why I write these things when I am absent, that when I come, I may not have to be harsh in my use of authority—the authority the Lord gave me for building you up, not for tearing you down. Finally, brothers and sisters, rejoice! Strive for full restoration, encourage one another, be of one mind, live in peace. And the God of love and peace will be with you" (NIV).

The world as we know it does not seem to be getting any better, and it probably won't. Those who know me know that I am generally a very optimistic person, but I can see how reading the last sentence might make me sound more pessimistic than optimistic, which is far from the truth. During the time in which we find ourselves, I am prayerfully hopeful that more people will come to know the Lord and walk in step with Him. I believe now more than ever that the church can be the greatest and most beautiful healing agent this world has ever seen. We simply have to get our act together, which is a lot easier said than done, I know, but by the grace of God I know it can happen. It starts by getting back to the heart of the matter, and that is Christ.

I know there will be some who interject and say, "But what about doctrine? Doesn't that matter?" The obvious answer to that question is yes. I don't know of a biblically-sound teacher or pastor who would say otherwise. For what we believe about Jesus, the church and the afterlife is of great importance, but it does not help us or anyone to enter into the presence of God. To my knowledge, doctrine never saved anyone. It may deepen our understanding of what the Father has done for us in Christ, but it is not what saves us. It is not what draws us near. Let us remember what brought us to God in the first place, the Spirit's conviction and kindness entering into the chambers of our hearts. The Apostle Paul informs us in the book of Romans that it is God's kindness that leads us to repentance (Romans 2:4). There is a giant conviction in my own soul to live out what the Lord has graciously done in my life. Today, many skeptics hound us Christians for not living consistent lives, and, to an extent, what they're saying holds great truth. But here I submit to you a quote from the book Bad Christian Wonderful Savior:

"Let's just be blunt. The very definition of a hypocrite fits every Christian. And that's not a bad thing. Sinful people being saved by a sinless Savior brings glory to Jesus, and last time I checked we are only supposed to be pointing to His glory anyway. The only bad form of hypocrisy so to speak is when someone says 'I don't struggle' or 'I am a really awesome person' or 'look at my works' or tries to be holier-than-thou and simultaneously never says things like 'Lord have mercy on me, a sinner' or 'what a wretch I am' or 'God's strength is made perfect in my weakness.'"

Yes, it's true, I am that hypocrite as well, but how much more amazing is the God of the universe for loving a hypocrite like me in spite of it? God is not stupid. He knew that his sons and daughters would fall flat on their faces, the same way babies fall on their faces when they are first learning to walk. The interesting fact is that as Christians we are always learning to walk with the Lord, and, yes, that means we will fall on our faces time and time again. We may graduate from spiritual milk to spiritually solid meat, but that does not mean that we become bulletproof from making mistakes or falling short. And, to be fair, I don't believe that even the most notorious atheists keep their own morals and standards perfectly each and every moment of every day. It would be impossible, and, furthermore, we don't spend each and every waking moment with them, and we don't know what flows through their minds and hearts on a given day. Of course, they aren't held to the same standards that Christians are. So, when they do fall short, it seems like nobody gives a rip. Yet, when a Christian falls short and does something that isn't God-honoring, such as giving someone the middle finger in traffic, everyone is suddenly beside themselves. Double standard much?

Why do people freak out, though, when Christians do something that is counter to what they profess to believe? It is because we are meant to live above reproach (Philippians 2:15). To live in the heart of it all is to live a life of repentance and to live in the fruit of the Spirit (Galatians 5:22). Yet the only real way we can accomplish this is by being connected to the vinedresser. John 15 speaks these words to us:

"I am the true vine, and my Father is the vinedresser. Every branch in me that does not bear fruit he takes away, and every branch that does bear fruit he prunes, that it may bear more fruit. Already you are clean because of the word that I have spoken to you. Abide in me, and I in you. As the branch cannot bear fruit by itself, unless it abides in the vine, neither can you, unless you abide in me. I am the vine; you are the branches. Whoever abides in me and I in him, he it is that bears much fruit, for apart from me you can do nothing. If anyone does not abide in me, he is thrown away like a branch and withers; and the branches are gathered, thrown into the fire, and burned" (ESV).

At the core, we Christians are meant to reflect Christ, thus the vinedresser has to prune and cut away the things that don't produce fruit or life. It might seem harsh or cruel that God would simply do away with the branches that do not produce vitality, but if we are truly honest with ourselves, we do the same thing, and we have very little afterthought about it. I was watching a small clip of a woman pruning a tree, and what stunned me the most was that she said the branch she was pruning had no purpose and that it had to go. She had no attachment to the dead branch; she knew that it wasn't good for the rest of the tree. This can be interpreted (I believe) in one or two ways. The first way we can interpret God pruning or cutting off the dead branches is by viewing it as people who claim to be spiritually regenerate but really are not.

In short, these are people who claim to be followers of Jesus, who have stored up much knowledge in their minds, but nothing has made its way to the heart. I'm sure that this doesn't sit well with some and even seems very crude; however, in some ways, this can be a healthy way of referencing where we are. Let's look at the classic verse in Matthew 7:15-21:

"Beware of false prophets. They come to you in sheep's clothing, but inwardly they are ravenous wolves. By their fruit you will recognize them. Are grapes gathered from thorn bushes, or figs from thistles? Likewise, every good tree bears good fruit, but a bad tree bears bad fruit. A good tree cannot bear bad fruit, and a bad tree cannot bear good fruit. Every tree that does not bear good fruit is cut down and thrown into the fire. So then, by their fruit you will recognize them. Not everyone who says to Me, 'Lord, Lord,' will enter the kingdom of heaven, but only he who does the will of My Father in heaven. Many will say to Me on that day, 'Lord, Lord, did we not prophesy in Your name, and in Your name drive out demons and perform many miracles?' Then I will tell them plainly, 'I never knew you; depart from Me, you workers of lawlessness'" (ESV).

The key to this passage is bearing good fruit. The question that then arises is, how does one bear good fruit, spiritually speaking? Short answer: by being connected to the heavenly vinedresser. This means that we spend time daily in His presence, however that plays out for us on a given day. The key here is being wrapped up in how much God loves us, truly allowing His love for us to manifest in all areas of our lives. Brennan Manning would say it in far simpler terms:

"Define yourself radically as one beloved by God. This is the true self. Every other identity is illusion." In every paper that was ever submitted by me for various psychology formats, I have always come back to the understanding that we are all first made in the image of God and therefore have vast amounts of love, dignity, and self-worth. Perhaps it's only my perception, but it seems as though we believers in Christ get easily entangled in the understanding that we have to do things and work hard for God to love, adore, and delight in us. This makes me think of when Jesus was led into the desert to be tempted by Satan. It was in this time that Satan would taunt the Lord Jesus and make statements like, "If you are God…" but Jesus, being calm and secure in His own identity, was all but saying, "I know who I am; I know whom I belong to; and I don't need to prove myself to you." And, to put further emphasis on Jesus' self-understanding, He says in John 10:30, "I and the father are one" (ESV). And another time, in John 14:9, Jesus tells Phillip, "Whoever has seen me has seen the father" (ESV).

## Question for Reflection

Do you ever find yourself forgetting the heart of the Gospel? In that God has loved madly in Christ, what can you do in your life to not lose sight of that?

# 2
# Seeing God Is Seeing Love

> "But the man who is not afraid to admit everything that he sees to be wrong with himself, and yet recognizes that he may be the object of God's love precisely because of his shortcomings, can begin to be sincere. His sincerity is based on confidence, not in his own illusions about himself, but in the endless, unfailing mercy of God."
>
> Thomas Merton, *No Man Is an Island*

IT IS never enough to see Jesus as a good moral teacher or prophet, for a good moral teacher could not perform the miracles that Jesus did while on this earth or have the spiritual authority that He possessed unless He had some divine authority given to Him. Though Jesus had all authority in His person, He was as fierce as a lion and as calm and tender as a dove. To say it again, Jesus was the direct reflection of our heavenly Abba. In my opinion, what prevents us from seeing the face of love the most is seeing the Father's wrath within the pages of the Old Testament. Many times, believers and skeptics alike react out of emotion rather than gaining a true understanding of what is going on.

For example, most people, including some Christians, believe that how God speaks and acts in the Old Testament is fundamentally different from the New Testament. Upon first glance, it might seem that way, but again we must gain a deeper understanding of what is going on. If you find yourself horrified or shocked at the fact that God would wipe out an entire group of people or city, that's probably a good sign because that means that your emotional faculties are working properly. I, too, have had that same reaction when my mind and heart began to engage the pages of Scripture, but what helped me understand and come to grips with what God does in the pages of Scripture as a whole was when I began to see things from the perspective of a father.

Mind you, I am not a father at this point and time in my life, but, if I am ever given the honor and pleasure, my son or daughter will know that their father will protect them as much as he possibly can from the forces of evil. If a man or group of men came into my home late at night and wanted more than simply appliances, but wanted to use my family for their evil purposes, you can rest assured that I would meet this force of evil with much fire and resistance of my own, even if it meant taking their lives. Would I enjoy it? Most certainly not, but if wiping out a group of wicked and evil people who threatened the peace and well-being of my family was necessary, I would do it. Much of the same motivation, I believe, can be said of God the Father in protecting both the Israelites and Gentiles of today. God wants to protect us from anything that aims to attack the holiness and purity that He has graciously bestowed upon us. I'm sure that it can be difficult to believe that God could love us this much, but if it's true, then we have to let it move from our brains to our hearts.

We have to let it transform our lives from the inside out. We have to allow God to love us and let His love move over the old scars and pains in our lives. And, in no shortage of words, we must have God as our first love before anything else in our lives. This never truly made sense to me until I realized that nothing else in this world could provide me with the kind of love that my heart desires the way God can. That doesn't mean that I don't desire a relationship with a woman and a future wife someday or even kids of my own. But when there are human beings mixed in the fold, where sin abounds, feelings get hurt, hearts get broken, and relationships fracture. Yet God is there to love us the way we have always wanted. Again, simply because we have God (the King of the universe) as our ultimate love, it does not in any way mean that we don't take chances on loving people. But we must not make others our ultimate satisfaction.

Only when we know how much God loves us can we truly love others. When we see how God loves us in our stubbornness, we can begin to love others on their own. Only when we see how much God loves us in our selfishness can we love others on their own. The price and risk that our Lord took, despite what stubborn and selfish people we are, to provide us with new hearts, minds, hands, and feet, is something that is so marvelous that no metaphor or a new way of understanding will ever compare to how wide and deep the love of God is for us. Still, though, the question stands: How do we allow God to love us? After all, it's not that easy, yet I believe that there is great freedom in admitting such an honest statement. It's strange to me how skeptics largely assume that they're the only ones who have questions. All one would have to do is look inside the mind of an honest-thinking Christian to know that we have questions, too.

The only difference is that Christians are not afraid to approach God with our questions, for we know that our questions will not move God's eyes from us but only bring us closer to Him if we allow them to. Hebrews 11:6 tells us, "And without faith it is impossible to please God because anyone who comes to him must believe that he exists and that he rewards those who earnestly seek him" (NIV). Of course, after reading the above passage, it would be very easy to think, "Well, I barely even believe that God exists," which is a perfectly okay statement and conclusion to make, but I believe what must be examined and focused on is the small seed of faith that it takes to make such a statement. If you barely believe that God exists, that suggests, then, that there is a small spark inside you that has the ability to be ignited.

## Question for Reflection

What in your life is keeping you from seeing God's love for you? What do you need to lay aside and repent of?

# 3
# Letting Abba Ignite the Spark

> "Do not marvel that I said to you, 'You must be born again.'"
> John 3:7 (ESV)

SOMETIMES, in order to see the truth, the heart has to first soften. The greatest example I can give you is from my own life. I was born with cerebral palsy, so I was given a very small chance to live. My birth weight was four pounds and four ounces. Doctors told my parents double-sided news, meaning that, on one hand, the doctor told them that I'd grow out of the condition, but, on the other hand, that I'd never be able to ride a bike or even clothe myself. I'd always be dependent on someone for my needs. With having cerebral palsy came a myriad of operations on my body. My spine was first, then came a hamstring lengthening in both my legs; both of my hips were medically broken and cut in half in order that both my feet could have arch support in them. For a time, I had metal plates in both my hips, and any time that I would roll over on either side, they would make a loud pop.

Each operation would take over a year of recovery time; physical therapy was also included in that. For so long, what stuck with me the most was the amount of pain that came with each operation. When I had my spine operated on, after about an hour of being awake, my surgeon came in with some physical therapists. He informed me that it was time to sit up, meaning that my feet had to hang over the edge of the bed. Even as a nurse elevated my bed slightly, it felt as though someone was attempting to rip my flesh apart. It took a few nurses and the physical therapists to pull me to the side of the bed where my feet hung over. I can almost hear myself screaming in pain as a kid in my head even now. Despite the pain, I am extremely grateful for my family, my doctor who provided me the ability to use my trunk properly, and all of the physical therapists who helped me get stronger in recovery.

The experience with getting both hamstrings lengthened was about the same; after about an hour of post-surgery recovery time, in came my doctor with some physical therapists. One of the therapists brought with her a small walker, and when my eyes locked on to what she'd brought along with her, my small frame began to tremble. I knew what was about to take place; the physical therapists, nurses, and even my parents would have to get me out of my hospital bed and in a standing position in the walker that the nurse had brought in. I'm not sure that there are enough words to describe what shot through my legs when my feet touched the floor. I remember wanting to collapse to the floor, but I heard the voice of my doctor saying that I had to try and stand up straight. He might have even told me to try and take a few steps, but the exact details are lost to my recollection.

These two separate times in my life sometimes feel as if they are all one; they very much shaped my view of God, which was that He was a cruel, cold-hearted, sick excuse for a deity that liked to watch people suffer. Of course, that isn't how I feel now, but for a good part of my life, this was my disposition toward the grand Creator of the universe. It took a while for my hard heart to begin to slowly turn in a new direction. All along, though, I now know that God was there, slowly and tenderly turning my face toward His. Before encountering this tender lion, I was a very sad and lonely kid who didn't have much self-worth at all. As such, there was much time spent trying to find that worth in my peers.

## Letting Abba Ignite the Spark

I would lie about being in a rock band or make up extravagant stories in order for people to like me. Worse yet, I didn't have much respect for the opposite sex. The simplest way to say it is that I felt like my own life was meaningless, and therefore their lives were meaningless as well. In spite of all of this, there was a deep sense that there was a divine spark beginning to ignite inside me. I began to feel and believe that there was more to life than the pursuit of my pleasures, and somewhere inside me, I wanted there to be more than a pitch-black afterlife when I died, where only my bones remained. Even though there was a longing for my life to be over, there was also a longing to live. On the last day of my senior year of high school, all the seniors gathered for our senior picnic. As usual, I kept to myself and sat with the one friend that I did have. We both devoured the burgers and hot dogs that were on our paper plates. We both made small talk through the chewing of food, but all I could think of doing was going home and getting lost in the music that I loved.

On top of that, there was still a long and drawn-out war taking place inside me, yet as cliché as it is, I felt as though Heaven and Hell were waging war for my soul. There was still a part of me that wanted to live, and there was a part of me that wanted to die. It was at the senior picnic that I would meet my friend Garret. He came into my life wearing a white t-shirt that had the word Revolution on the front, black windbreaker pants, Adidas shoes, a blue hat that he wore backwards, and dreadlocks that rested underneath. I was instantly intrigued, to say the least. I was walking out to the parking lot when our paths crossed. At that time in my life, there was a habit that I had where I would start talking to people and not first introduce myself. I did the same with Garret. I asked him what his shirt meant; he told me it was the name of his youth group.

Automatically, there were alarms being tripped inside me because, again, there was a longing inside me (a spark if you will) for something that the life I was existing in was not offering. When he told me that it was a church youth group that he attended, I began to hold my breath because, the truth of the matter is, I was in shock. There were a few possibilities in my mind as to what could be going on. Either this was a simple coincidence that my mind was simply putting together, or this was the God that created the heavens and the earth that was reaching out to me. I decided to believe that this was God reaching out to me, but I wasn't sure what to expect, and there was plenty of anger and hostility inside me that had to be dealt with. As I got to know Garret over the following summer, what impressed me the most about him was his ability to listen and his ability to show compassion. My parents liked him and grew to trust him pretty quickly.

They even allowed him to take me to his youth group on a Wednesday night, and going there was like someone going into a home of complete strangers. Garret stuck by me the remainder of the night, and people were warm and friendly, but still, there was the feeling of being a complete outcast in such a place as this. What would God want with someone like me, a filthy-mouthed punk kid who still had his fists clenched in God's presence? With Garret in my life now, though, there was something so disarming about him. Often, after youth group, we would go out to eat, or we would sit and talk somewhere. This was one of the first times that I experienced real friendship in my life.

After a few weeks of spending time with Garret, there was still a great stubbornness that resided inside me. But the more time I spent time with Garret, the more my hard heart began to soften to the Lord's presence. One night, when I was at Revolution, the youth pastor was talking about having a covenant relationship with God. As the sermon went on, I began to feel overwhelmed with love. No longer could I deduce this moment as mere chemicals going through my body. I had never felt this way before in my life. When the youth pastor finished his sermon, I walked up to him after waiting in a line of other people. When it was my turn, I again started talking to him without properly introducing myself. I remember that the first thing I said to him was, "I don't have that relationship with God that you were talking about." I can remember sitting there with the youth pastor, telling him that I knew that I needed God, but that I didn't know why God would make me in such a way, meaning that I had to live with cerebral palsy when I wanted to be like everyone else. After I was finished telling the youth pastor these things about me, he put his arm gently around me and said, "You know why I think God made you this way? Because He knew you could handle it."

At first, the answer didn't suffice, but as I look back on my life, if that was in fact one reason that God allowed me to live with this condition, then it makes sense to me because I have (by the grace of God) done more with life having cerebral palsy then I probably would have done as an abled-bodied person. Having cerebral palsy has allowed me the privilege to connect and relate to others in personal ways. Having cerebral palsy has revealed to me my deep-seated need to connect with Abba's love in a way that I probably wouldn't have as an able-bodied person. I know my heart well enough to know that if I was able to walk, run, and do all the things that any normal person can do, I'd probably not give a crap about people as I do now, I'd probably be much more self-absorbed than I am now, and I'd probably not be seeking the Lord each and every day with my life as I try and do on a daily basis.

Of course, this does not mean that a person with cerebral palsy or any other condition couldn't give the middle finger to God and turn the other way. Lots of people do this every day, regardless of physical ability or lack thereof. All I'm saying is that for me, having this condition has allowed me to draw near to God in rich and intimate ways. In many ways, the heartbeat of all these pages is knowing how deeply, richly, and intimately God loves you and wants to be with you. The late Brennan Manning has been a significant resource in discovering, once again, how much God loves not only me but all of His sons and daughters. Each and every day I can't begin to tell you the number of times that I forget more often than remember that God loves me. It's so easy to forget and all the easier to believe that God hates me and thinks that I'm a worthless piece of crap.

I believe that if ever there was a time when Christians need to remember again how much love God has given us, it's now. As I said previously, the world seems to be spinning out of control, and it doesn't appear as if it's going to get any better. I've never been one who is crazy about the end times, and over the last several years, various groups have claimed that we are in the end times. Yet, Scripture tells us that we won't know the time (Mark 13:32), but if I were ever in a time in which Jesus was going to return, I would want to be consciously aware of my standing in Christ because of the love He poured out for me. It's the only thing that would matter—that and what I did with His love.

As I mentioned in previous pages, when it came to engaging friends in my life who have chosen not to believe or share in the same beliefs as I do, I would clam up and not know how to articulate a thoughtful response to their questions or comments. More so, what would happen was that my heart would become so heavy that I would simply want to cry out to the person about how much God loved them and how much they mattered to Him. I know that my response would be out of pure emotion, but it would be true, nonetheless. But this is the spark that I am referring to, that spark that God slowly ignites, which grows into a bright fire. It is when we allow Abba to ignite the spark within us that we can begin to see Him working within us and allowing us to bring about change in our world and within ourselves. This spark is by grace and faith alone.

Sometimes, though, if we're not careful, the flame inside can die out. I don't believe that this means that we lose our salvation, although it can certainly feel that way. The point is that we need to be careful to

## Letting Abba Ignite the Spark

dwell daily in the Lord's love for us, lest we forget and wander off to paths that we were never meant to embark on. God only knows that I have done this all too many times. Spending the last four years of my college career at a faith-based college, I have found them to be the most challenging for my faith. There were many times where I felt as though the faith that I once had was slipping away. Instead of dwelling on God's richness of love, grace, and mercy toward me, I would get caught up in matters of theology and the vast theological positions, to the point that I began to lose sight of what mattered most, that is, the love God has for me and everyone.

When this happens, the flame is fully put out, and love dies. Michael C. Patton would also call this spiritual depression. I don't know how else to describe this, other than that the God you once thought you knew appears to be a million miles from you. Your mind feels like it's caught in an endless storm, and the only thing that sounds reasonable to you is the grave. I'm not trying to be dramatic or play on people's emotions. I literally felt like I was going to die. I went to a few trusted professors at my college, and they are were extremely warm and kind, and some of their answers helped me, even. But what I needed most was love and presence. I would lie in my bed at my college dorm at night, and I would feel the tears stream down my face as I cried out to know the living God again. At this point in my journey, I was doubting everything, even my own salvation. I was looking for answers, but I never looked in God's love letter to me in the pages of Scripture, and I didn't put aside all the nonsense that filled my mind to remember who I am in God's sight.

Perhaps you can identify with a lot of what I'm sharing with you in these pages. The first point that I would like to establish is that we all fall short and we all struggle. The second point that I would like to establish is that at the end of time we will all stand before God and give an account of our lives. It will not matter the accolades that one has received over a lifetime or how wealthy a person can become in a lifetime. What will matter is how we responded to the love of our heavenly Abba. Have you welcomed Him into your life? Have you allowed Him to love you passionately, deeply, and madly? Or have you done everything in your human power to keep yourself occupied, to keep from even acknowledging that Abba's love for you is the love you have always wanted and longed for?

Accepting, knowing, and walking in the love of God has been the single greatest achievement of my earthly existence. His love is better than any rush a new relationship could provide, better than any comfort that alcohol or food could provide. And far better any sexual pleasure that I could experience. Why? Because they're all momentary, but God's love and adoration are always constant. It isn't as though He loves you one day and hates you the next. Sometimes, when we feel numb to life's circumstances, we try to find things that will make us feel, things that make us come alive. But the honest, raw truth is that nothing, not even good things, will make a flame ignite inside us the way the love of God can and will. It doesn't matter what you have done, no matter how bitter, frustrated, and hate-filled you are. It doesn't matter how many people you've slept with, how much drugs you've taken, what trail of broken relationships, failed marriages, or reputation that you have made for yourself. If you have but a single spark inside you that longs to encounter the living Abba, even with the tiniest spark, He'll turn it into the brightest flame.

## Question for Reflection

Think about the time when you felt God's love come crashing into you: What was that like? If you haven't felt God's love ignite the spark in your life, what's holding you back?

# 4
## Accept the Acceptance

"All that the Father gives me will come to me, and whoever comes to me I will never cast out."
John 6:37 (ESV)

I RECENTLY HEARD the phrase "accepting the acceptance" while listening to a talk by Brennan Manning. These words really stuck with me because, in my own life, I haven't truly accepted that I'm accepted. And that is so strange to me because our heavenly Abba gave up His beloved Son as a sacrifice for our sins and those of all who would put their faith and trust in Him. Jesus, the beloved, also gave up His position next to His Father to take on human flesh in order to walk among us humans. Sounds strange and even bizarre, doesn't it? Why would God give up His only Son in order to redeem those whom He calls beloved sons and daughters? Why have your only son slaughtered on a cross? What is so special about us humans, anyway? Honestly, there is nothing truly special about any of us, other than the fact that we are made in God's image. Apart from that, we are wretched people who choose our own way. Yet Jesus paints for us the single greatest picture in the history of all pictures. This picture is found in Luke 15:11-32. This story speaks of a younger brother who simply wants the inheritance that he will get when his father dies. Rather than living in a relationship with his father until his father dies, the son wants the inheritance now. He feels entitled and feels that his father owes him his inheritance. When the younger son gets ahold of the money, he then blows all of it in a swift manner. To make things hit home a bit more, think of someone who gets their hands on a lot of money and ends up spending all of the money on all that their heart desires, but they still end up feeling empty and with nothing to show for it.

This is essentially what happens to the younger son. He burns through all his money, and when he comes to his senses, he thinks, "There's no way my father will allow me back into his home… What have I done? I have disgraced my father and his legacy." When you read the story, you can feel the regret and shame shoot through the veins of the younger son. After the son comes to his senses, he decides to go back to his father and basically say that he deserves to be moved to a position of a slave or hired servant. Let's take a few moments and allow this to sink in and move in you.

Here the son wants to go from the position of a beloved son to a servant. I believe that when it comes to our own relationship with the Father, it is difficult to know deep in our stomachs that we are accepted as beloved sons and daughters. Personally, I believe that I am better off being allowed to wash the feet of God on a daily basis than to be an actual son, fully accepted into the kingdom of grace. Some of us who cling to the name and personhood of Christ actually have ozone layer-like doubts that God really loves us. Instead, we might even feel that God is ready to boot us out of Heaven at any moment because we've blown it way too many times. We just can't seem to get our acts cleaned up quickly enough. We can't break the addictive drug cycle, we can't seem to break our grip on lustful desires, we don't attend church regularly, we don't, we don't. we don't. But what we fail to realize is that when all of those "we don't" statements creep into our minds, we are forgetting grace and who we have become in Christ Jesus. The simple fact that our minds and hearts tell us—that we must work harder to be accepted by the Father—is a bald-faced lie that is produced directly from the mouth of Satan.

When the younger son works his way home, little does he know that his father has been standing outside the front door of his home, looking and scanning for any trace of him. I can only imagine what the father must have been feeling; his heart must have felt as though there were a thousand breaks weighing on it. He must have been holding back a wealth of tears behind his eyes as well. Yet when he sees his younger son from a distance, he takes off sprinting toward him. He is so delighted to see his son that the furthest thing from his mind is how his son has demanded something that wasn't his to have yet and how deeply he has been disrespected and sinned against by his son. Quite the opposite happens—the father wraps his arms around the neck of his son and kisses him over and over.

I can guarantee you the younger son did not expect his father to react in this way; rather, he was expecting his father to look at him sternly and with much disappointment and demand that he leave his sight at once. The shock and even confusion are real when his father grips him tightly and kisses him nonstop. When the father finally lets go and stops kissing his son, the son looks at him and speaks of his desire to be hired on as a slave, but his father doesn't buy it, and it doesn't appear to cross his mind. Instead, he places a ring on his son's hand, dresses him in fine clothing, and calls for a celebration of epic proportions. There is something inside me (if I'm honest) that longs to be this younger son, in that I would have loved to experience God the Father rejoicing over me in this way, so much that he places a beautiful ring on his son's finger, clothes him in fine attire, and has a magnificent party for him. I don't even know how I would even begin to comprehend that as one person; much of the same could be said for the body of Christ.

The father loves his son so deeply, passionately, and madly. Do we believe that God loves us this much? Do I believe that God loves me this much? Do we believe that God loves our unbelieving friends this much? I don't think so; as I've stated before, I believe most of us believe that God is ready to break His foot off in our backsides, that He has a flippant temper and is ready to fly off the handle when we sin. And, when it comes to our friends who don't believe the same as we do, do we believe that God beckons for their hearts on an hourly and even daily basis? I think that some of us long for our friends and loved ones to know Christ, but we don't believe that the Father will move Heaven and earth to draw them near. We might feel the same about them as we do ourselves, that God is simply willing to throw them to the wayside. More often than not, we believe the deep lie inside our hearts, rather than what Scripture actually says, that the Father wouldn't want anyone to perish, but everyone to come to repentance (2 Peter 3:9).

The problem, then, lies more in our own hearts and personal dispositions than it does in God. God is perfect and has no insecurity in Himself and what He can do. Rather, He wants us as beloved sons and daughters to interact and engage with Him in faith, believing that He is good and trustworthy. When we can reach a point where we accept that we are accepted by the Father, we will sense the mad love of the Father sinking deep into our veins. We will feel a love that we have never known before, we will sense bravery rise up inside us that was never there before, and, lastly, the mad love of the Father will move us to love others in ways we never could—love that simply is and with no strings attached.

The Apostle Paul was the greatest example of accepting the acceptance. In Romans 8:38-39, Paul speaks the beautiful words:

"For I am convinced that neither death nor life, neither angels nor principalities, neither the present nor future, nor any powers, neither height nor depth, nor anything else in all creation, will be able to separate us from the love of God that is in Christ Jesus our Lord" (BSB).

In the Bible, the Apostle Paul is a man who knows that he is fully accepted by God. Even in spite of great suffering, his trust in the mad love of the Father is ruthless. The love and acceptance that Paul speaks of are not something that we have to embark on a spiritual pilgrimage for, though that is most often the case. I have known a few people in my life, who, just by opening the pages of Scripture, have come to know Christ as Lover and Lord of their souls. In my own life and experience, I have gone through Buddhism, agnosticism, and, finally, reached falling for the mad love of Christ.

Yet, if I'm honest, I am that prodigal son. I wander off from the Father's presence. I am always so stunned that he takes me back so quickly and without reservations. This morning as I woke up, I sensed a deep yearning for the Lord's presence, so I opened up the pages of Scripture, and still, everything seemed to be as dry as a desert. As such, my spirit went to its default thought process, in which I had to earn God's attention and affections. Yet, I knew that nothing I could do would ever make Abba love me any more or any less. When I was in the bathroom, of all places, relieving myself of bodily waste, it was there on the toilet that I heard the words whispered inside me, "You don't have to beg for my attention, son." Automatically, I had a vision of a helpless child crying on a floor and their parent coming to pick them up just as they reached their tiny arms out for their love and affection. God is much the same. All we must do is stretch our arms out, and He will be there to pick us up off the floor. Accept that you are accepted by the Father.

## Question for Reflection

Deep down inside, have you really accepted that you are truly accepted by and in Christ?

# 5
# When Jesus Enters Your Home

> "Our hearts are restless until they rest in you."
> St. Augustine of Hippo, *Confessions*

IN LUKE CHAPTER 7, there is a story of a Roman officer who at the time had a servant who was deathly ill. The officer was a lover of the Jewish community, so much that he had built a synagogue for them. What caught my attention in this story is that when he sent some Jewish elders out to get the attention of Jesus, Jesus made his way to the Roman officer to heal his servant, but the officer said, "Lord, don't trouble yourself by coming to my home, for I am not worthy of such an honor. I am not even worthy to come and meet you. Just say the word from where you are, and my servant will be healed. I know this because I am under the authority of my superior officers, and I have authority over my soldiers. I only need to say, 'Go,' and they go, or 'Come,' and they come. And if I say to my slaves, 'Do this,' they do it" (NLT).

Jesus was amazed at the officer's faith, and when the man returned home, his servant was healed and restored to health. What strikes me the most is the officer's reaction to Jesus wanting to come to his home and how the officer first doesn't want to trouble Jesus, and secondly, he doesn't feel worthy enough to meet Jesus face to face. This man's personal disposition reveals a lot. In the officer's first response of not wanting to trouble Jesus to come to heal his servant in a personal way, that kind of thinking often can reflect how we feel about our own intimate relationship with the Father. Even knowing that I can call the Maker of the Heavens and earth "Daddy," there are still plenty of times when I feel like I'm bothering God with my same old prayers, complaints, and frustrations. Many times, I feel like a homeless drug addict who has been in and out of a recovery center and can't seem to get it together. Sometimes, the inside of my heart and mind is like that of a person who has a serious hoarding problem. There's junk everywhere.

As a result, I can greatly relate to how this Roman officer feels when he tells Jesus to not trouble himself by coming to his home. If it was me, I'd say, "Oh no, Jesus, You don't want to come to my house; it's a mess." What the officer is trying to do with these responses is, he is trying to create a distance between himself and Jesus, the same way that Adam and Eve did with themselves and God in the garden. They were both naked and did not want God to see them that way. I don't know what sins populated the heart and mind of the Roman officer, but I know that our sin is not enough to keep the mad love of Christ away from us.

In Luke 19, there is a man name Zacchaeus, who was the chief tax collector and also very wealthy. The passage tells us that he was short in stature. One day, when he heard that Jesus was in his area, he tried to get his eyes on Jesus, and since he was short in stature, he had to climb up a tree in order to see Him. Since he was such a wealthy man, it seems out of place that a rich man would climb a tree. He probably could have hired people to carry him on some lofty contraption of some form. That way, he could have relaxed wherever he went and been able to see everything. But I believe that his willingness to climb a tree reveals to us a rather large hint about what was going on inside of his heart. Later on in the passage, we're told that the people around Jesus were "displeased" when Jesus called upon Zacchaeus because He wanted to be a guest in his home. In my estimation, I believe that Zacchaeus was growing weary of the life that he was leading. Maybe he had grown tired of his greedy self that took more money than he should have from the people in his community. Regardless of how we might feel about people like Zacchaeus, I believe we can all relate to him, in that we all have something inside of us that haunts us. For him, maybe it was his greed, his ability to take advantage of others to elevate himself. Maybe people in his community thought he could never change. Maybe he even heard people say that about him in passing; maybe people even gossiped about him.

Perhaps Zacchaeus knew that there was no way he could change on his own. Maybe he realized that no amount of positive thinking or behavior modification could change his heart. And so, climbing up in that tree to see and be seen by Jesus was the only way he knew he could change. Those who were displeased with Jesus going into the home of Zacchaeus probably didn't realize that this was the same Jesus who was called a glutton, drunkard, and a friend of tax collectors and sinners (Matthew 11:9). It's interesting that people in Jesus' community would imply that Jesus was a friend of sinners because Jesus Himself said, "Healthy people don't need a doctor--sick people do. I have come to call not those who think they are righteous, but those who know they are sinners" (Mark 2:17, NLT).

Zacchaeus knew deep down in his bowels that he was a sinner, and what sets him apart from the Roman officer is that he wasn't afraid to be seen by Jesus. He wasn't afraid to let Christ into his home. You might even call it faith. I don't know what the inside of Zacchaeus's home looked like, but there was something inside him that wasn't afraid to let Jesus see. And if inside the home of Zacchaeus was a mess, it wasn't enough to draw Jesus away from him. In Jewish communities, having a meal with someone or wanting to be a guest in someone's home is a way of saying that you want to have a relationship with a person or family. With the religious leaders of Jesus' time, not only would they have been repulsed because Jesus went into a home of a sinner, but that Jesus would actually sit next to a sinner. Religiously zealous people would probably want Jesus to sit far away from someone like Zacchaeus, and the only possible way that Zacchaeus could be around Jesus was when and if he cleaned up his act. Jesus rebuked these religious leaders strongly. When He was sitting down to eat, He didn't do a ceremonial hand washing, and when the religious leaders questioned His actions, Jesus said this in response:

"Woe to you, teachers of the law and Pharisees, you hypocrites! You clean the outside of the cup and dish, but inside they are full of greed and self-indulgence" (NIV). Again, the difference here is that Zacchaeus is willing to admit his own brokenness. He's willing to say that he has a messy home (internally speaking), that his heart is out of order, and isn't centered on the heart of Abba. Jesus wants to come into your home, no matter how messy or disorganized it is. He wants to take up residence in your mind and in your heart, now and forever. He will take the disorganized and cluttered lives we call our homes and help us to make sense of and place things in proper order. He will immerse every area of our lives with such a sweet love, better than any earthly romance we could ever fathom.

## Question for Reflection

Do you feel as though your spiritual heart (your home) would be ready for Christ to enter? What are some things that you can do to ready it for him?

# 6
# He Delights

> "The Lord your God is in your midst,
> a mighty one who will save;
> he will rejoice over you with gladness;
> he will quiet you by his love;
> he will exult over you with loud singing."
> Zephaniah 3:17 (ESV)

A FEW DAYS AGO, when I opened up my inbox, I received a daily devotional from Max Lucado. The title of the devotional was, "God is Crazy About You." I opened the email with much anticipation, and what stuck out to me the most were the two verses that Pastor Lucado included in the devotional. The first one was Psalm 18:19:

"He brought me out into a spacious place; he rescued me because he delighted in me" (NIV). The second was Isaiah 62:5b:

"as a bridegroom rejoices over his bride, so will your God rejoice over you" (NIV). The words "delight" and "rejoice" are obscure words to me; they have been hard for me to accept. Even though I wrote earlier that we have to accept the acceptance, I confess that it is still hard for me, and, more often than not, I have to start over at square one with knowing that I am a beloved son of the highest and glorious Abba. C.S. Lewis said it best when he said, "Relying on God has to begin all over again every day as if nothing had yet been done." Every morning, it's as though I have to say, "Abba, please enlighten me to the truth of who I am in You once again," because in this endless assault we call life, our mental life, in particular, can become overfilled with doubt, discouragement, and despair.

## A Mad Love & A Shameless Audacity

I am often reminded of just how much I don't have it together, but then I am reminded of how much God loves me. Yet, the question that arises in my heart is, do I love Him back in return? Does my heart respond and leap with joy knowing how much He loves me? From my own life, I can say that the answer is no, in that I am more often than not faced with my flaws, I am also extremely hard on myself, and I have the ability to mess things up at times. I burn mental and emotional energy dwelling on these things instead of on how madly the Father has loved me. I am more apt to say that God is displeased with me, rather than that He delights over me. Further into the devotional, Pastor Max Lucado shared these words "If God had a refrigerator, your picture would be on it. If he had a wallet, your photo would be in it." Honestly, I still have a hard time believing this, even after a simple copy and paste into a word document. It gives more emphasis to the phrase "too good to be true." If there really is a heavenly Abba who loves us so madly, it's only logical for me to believe that there is an enemy that hates us (those who believe and place our love and trust on the heart of Abba). This enemy (in my opinion) would do all he could to thwart our belief that the heavenly Father loved us, or that we were even worth taking the chance on.

Scripture tells us that there is an enemy and that he is the father of lies (John 8:44). The interesting fact is that the lies of the enemy are carefully woven with some truth. In my own life, the lies move through my mind and heart like deadly cancer, destroying every good cell in my body. Only this cancer is more spiritual and cannot be cured with earthly medicine only. I have been on antidepressants for over ten years. I have seen a handful of different counselors, but nothing has helped me fight the deep cancerous lies of the enemy like the mad love of the Father. That doesn't mean that other mental health treatments don't work (they can), but that medicine and therapy alone cannot touch the spiritual realm in their own power. We must also realize that we are not merely physical, emotional, and spiritual beings in separate compartments. They all work as one. The physical can affect the emotional; the emotional can affect the spiritual; and so on and so forth.

Even knowledgeable mental health professionals understand that medicine is not enough, and so they employ different behavioral therapies to change our thinking. Again, this can work, but it won't touch our deepest spiritual brokenness and longings. The only real way we can know how and why the Father delights and dances over us is first being aware of the deepest, broken parts of ourselves. Many of us have a fear of taking a deep, long look at the wreckage that is our inner selves. But, if nothing can separate us from the love of the Father, what do we have to fear? (I'm speaking to those who already trust in the Father's love for them.) Some of us, though we have confessed Jesus as Savior and King, still haven't dealt with the darkest areas of ourselves. We have not shone the light of God's love, mercy, and truth upon them. It can be extremely difficult to admit the truth about ourselves aloud and all the more comforting to keep the truth inside us.

We may find ourselves thinking, "If God already knows everything about me, why do I have to share my guts with Him?" Yes, He already knows all about you, but what He longs for is intimacy with His beloved. Even though God already knows all, He rightfully can choose to stand far off from us, but in Christ Jesus His Son, He has chosen to come near to us. Scripture tells us that when one sinner repents, the angels rejoice (Luke 15:10). And, as we have seen with the story of the prodigal son, the father ran to his son, clenched his neck, and kissed him. In the same way, when we open the darkest chambers of ourselves to our heavenly Abba, we find that He rejoices, runs toward us, and kisses us the same way that the prodigal son's father did.

Yet, we must carefully understand that this is all by God's grace and grace alone. Because of His riches, He has drawn us to Himself. Scripture tells us we love because He first loved us (1 John 4:19).

Brennan Manning wrote the following words as a commentary to Psalm 23: "The God I've come to know by sheer grace... has furiously loved me regardless of my state—grace or disgrace. And why? For his love is never, never based on our performance, never conditioned by our moods—of elation or depression. The furious love of God knows no shadow of alternation or change. It is reliable. And always tender." I believe that one of the reasons that we resist the acceptance and delight that our wonderful Father has for us is because we are more in touch with our old selves so that we have the old self as a permanent form of identification. Saint Paul made war against this form of thinking when he wrote in 2 Corinthians 5:17 the famous words, "Therefore, if anyone is in Christ, the new creation has come: The old has gone, the new is here! All this is from God, who reconciled us to himself through Christ and gave us the ministry of reconciliation: that God was reconciling the world to himself in Christ, not counting people's sins against them. And he has committed to us the message of reconciliation. We are therefore Christ's ambassadors, as though God were making his appeal through us. We implore you on Christ's behalf: Be reconciled to God. God made him who had no sin to be sin for us so that in him we might become the righteousness of God" (NIV).

In an earthly sense, this is hard for me to imagine because I am a finite person, and, as I said before, I have an easier time seeing myself in the filthy rags of my own sin than through the lens of God's delight in me. But, in a spiritual and imaginative sense, I can clearly and easily see myself walking into the Lord's presence in a white robe, without stain and being able to walk without assistance. And God the Father wraps me in His arms and holds me tightly as He smiles with delight. For the last several years in my journey of trying to follow Jesus, I have heard from various pastors and fellow believers that when the Father looks at me, He sees His Son. What they mean by that is that the Father sees you and me (as believers) as holy, blameless, and spotless, the same way as

Jesus. And while that has brought me some comfort, I've begun to wonder recently if God actually sees me, His son, Brandon. As I said above, I have a much easier time believing that God sees me in the filth of my sin than in delight that I'm His son. Yet, as I have allowed myself time to sit and let Him show me His love through reading the Scriptures, and also in prayer and quiet stillness, I am ever moved by His love for me. When I allow myself to dwell in His presence, my spirit is moved with great joy that causes a smile to break out across my face. And, dare I say that the Father smiles down on me as well (the same can be said for you if you're trusting in Him and His love for you)? The Gospel of Saint John is a book that I have read countless times, and, as with many believers, I can read things over and over and miss the most important, the smallest and most powerful of truths.

For instance, when I was skimming through John Chapter 13, I began to read about Jesus predicting His betrayal as He was surrounded by his disciples. What jumped out to me in the most significant of ways were the following three verses:

"One of them, the disciple whom Jesus loved, was reclining next to him. Simon Peter motioned to this disciple and said, 'Ask him which one he means.' Leaning back against Jesus, he asked him, 'Lord, who is it?'" (NIV)

I know that it is easy to focus on the main topic, but to know the liberating intimacy that you have with our heavenly Abba through His beloved Son Jesus, focus on the intimacy in these few verses. John is reclining back on the heart of Jesus. And Jesus is allowing it without hesitation. Jesus didn't get weirded out because another man was lying against Him. I wonder if, as John was reclining back against Jesus, he felt Jesus' heartbeat as well. Or if he didn't feel the love of Jesus emanating out of His very being.

I love how the New King James version uses the word "bosom." I believe it captures the intimacy and beauty of the scene. Some scholars believe that John was the beloved, or that they were like best friends.

Knowing this makes my body surge with energy because I want that same connection with Jesus as John had. The deepest reality that we must understand is that Jesus died so that we can have that same relationship as John did with Him and vice versa. We are the beloved. In Jesus' death, burial, and resurrection, He has ripped down the barrier that our sin has put up. This was the Father's plan to not only attack that which keeps us away from Him (our sin), but He also longs to penetrate our hard hearts with how madly He loves His sons and daughters. He longs to show us His delight as we delight in Him in return.

## Question for Reflection

Do you believe that God actually delights in you? Or is that something that you wrestle with? How can you help somebody else see that God delights in them as well?

# 7
# The Old Man

> "Make war!"
> John Piper

SCRIPTURE TELLS US that we are a new creation in Christ Jesus; the old has gone, and the new has come (2 Corinthians 5:17-21). In recent days, when I'm reminded that I am a new creation in Christ, I imagine God sending a spiritual shock from our brains and all throughout the rest of our bodies, almost like a surgeon who has to reconnect certain nerve endings so that the rest of the body responds well. When you first experience the act of becoming a new creation, it's the most amazing gift a person could ever receive and have no idea they would have ever wanted it. And, when you do receive it, you don't want to let it go, almost like having a new lover in your life. All the feelings of passion and love; sometimes, you can't even imagine being away from the person.

And yet, in the deepest parts of ourselves, we experience that in the spiritual sense as well. When the Holy Spirit comes into our lives, our old desires fade away, and we have all new ones, ones that line up with who the Father is and who He wants us to be. When I first came to the knowledge that Father had chased me down with furious love, there was such thrill and excitement in the beginning; I thought that the thrill and rush would never go away; but, after a while, I would wake up the next morning feeling spiritually dry. I would read my Bible, and nothing would jump out or speak to me.

It was as though I was losing a new lover in my life; only this wasn't any new lover. This was the God of the world that surrounded me, and I wondered why He had left so quickly. Looking back on this specific time of my life, I realize that there was something inside me that relied on people or even the worship experience for the mere feeling of God's presence. After moments like these, I became disgruntled with myself and wondered if I was doing something wrong, or maybe I wasn't trying hard enough to please God. Of course, by now, though, we should know that it is through grace that we come to know our heavenly Abba, and there is not a single thing we could do to make Him love us more or less.

Yet, even when we have been spiritually shocked back to life, even when we have the desires to please the Father, even when we have desires to be among other fellow beloveds and see people come to know the deep love of the Father, there tends to be something of an old man (or former self) that can come lurking up from behind us when we least expect it. Ephesians 4:22-24 says this about the old self: "You were taught, with regard to your former way of life, to put off your old self, which is being corrupted by its deceitful desires; to be made new in the attitude of your minds; and to put on the new self, created to be like God in true righteousness and holiness" (NIV). Here is yet another rendering of the passage from the New Living Translation "throw off your old sinful nature and your former way of life, which is corrupted by lust and deception. Instead, let the Spirit renew your thoughts and attitudes. Put on your new nature, created to be like God—truly righteous and holy." I really love the NLT's rendering of the passage, probably because it speaks so richly to my own life, as it relates to lust and deception since these have both been areas that make up the old man that has lurked behind me for so long.

Many Reformed Protestants speak of making war against our fleshly desires and sin. I agree with this philosophy and understanding of combating our sin because anything that prevents us from being like Jesus must be dealt with directly. Yet, along with this truth, I've come to see that in my own hyper-vigilance toward my own sin, I forget that Jesus won the ultimate war against sin when He died upon the cross and was raised in victory from the tomb. Knowing that Christ fought the ultimate war against my sin should be the ultimate dose of freedom and joy, in that, He swung the ultimate kill shot to what only came to bring my death to my sin and former self.

Still, though, when glimpses of my former self appear, I am more eager to pick up the sword, rather than first remembering all that the Father has done for me through His beloved Son Jesus. What I am trying to say is that, in the midst of spiritual warfare, it is important that we do not fight back against the shadow of sin by our own might but by the power that the Spirit gives us.

The Open Chair

In following the previous chapter (the old man), we saw that, ultimately, spiritual warfare plays a part in combatting characteristics of the old man, or who we used to be. I noted that it is extremely important to know that Jesus was and is the ultimate spiritual warfare against our old selves and sin natures. In turn, this should provide us the freedom to breathe freely, knowing that we are new creations in Christ Jesus. One of the ways we raise the greatest defense against old habits that are destructive toward us is, I believe, by remembering all that the Father has done for us through His beloved Son Jesus. I'm in no way implying that we become lazy, lest we fall back into the arms of an old lover that was really no good to us in the first place. Yet, every soldier knows they have to leave their post in order to rest.

I believe it is all too possible to have all the Christian answers to all of life's hardest questions, and yet the soul can know no rest. The soul can still feel chained and held captive by memories of who you once were and mistakes that are not easily forgotten. In psychology, I learned about a type of therapy called "open chair therapy." In this practice, one places an open chair in front of them, and the chair can represent a conversation that you have not yet had with a friend or loved one, making one more ready for the conversation to take place. Or the open chair can represent a conversation with yourself when you were younger. I know it may seem odd talking to an empty chair; you could easily dismiss it as mere psychobabble and say that it would never have any benefit to your life in any way. Yet, in my own life, as I have used this practice, I have found great healing in my daily interactions with God and within myself. I first started using this practice one night in my college dorm; there were several moments in my childhood that have had a heavy impact on the mental and emotional areas of myself. For some reason, there was a moment in my childhood where I was leaning against the sink, attempting to help wash the dishes. In a moment of trying to be helpful, the glass I was washing fell out of my hands and shattered into the sink.

I can remember instantly feeling a sense of regret as I stood there looking at the glass that had shattered open. I remember my dad walking into the kitchen and saying, "It's okay," and after that, my mom coming over my opposite shoulder. I looked at her and said, "I was just trying to help." Even though she told me in reply that she wasn't mad, I've always felt that in that moment that she was, and ever since then, I have carried it with me. So there I was, sitting alone in my dorm room, and for some reason, I decided to lock my door. After I did that, I took a deep breath and sat on the floor with my now-empty chair facing me.

I quickly closed my eyes and imagined the smaller boy that was myself sitting in front of me. I tried as best I could to set aside how crazy this exercise seemed and began speaking to the younger version of myself. I closed my eye eyes and said, "Brandon, it's okay. You were only a kid and were only trying to help. You can let go of the shame you've carried." As I was speaking to a younger version of myself, I quickly realized that I was talking to myself in the here and now. The sting of tears began to trail down my face, and I quickly realized that the image of a little boy was now being replaced by an image of Jesus sitting in the chair, who was waiting for me to place my head in his lap. I have found that this was the purpose of the empty chair exercise so that I would learn to place my head in the lap of Christ. It's what all believers in Christ must do. We get so caught up in theology and who's wrong and who's right that we almost forget the freedom that we have been given in Christ. We forget to humble ourselves before Christ, knowing what we would be without Him. We forget to be as a child in faith before Him.

Jesus said, "Let the little children come to me." Think of how a child is when they are in complete trust of their mother and father.

They are without restraint, fear, hesitation, and doubt; they are full of joy and know that their mother and father have the best for them. This is exactly how we are meant to approach our heavenly Father, but many other things can get in the way of how we view the Father, such as our own fears, our own insecurities, doubts, longings, or whatever the case may be. We must do as Scripture says and be transformed by the renewing of our minds The only way that this can happen is by learning to rest our heads in the lap of Jesus every day. In my daily life, this plays out in two ways: one is by actually opening up God's truth and letting it sink deep in my life, and the second is actually lying down on the floor and picturing that I'm actually lying in the lap of Jesus.

It might seem silly to some, but for me, it has been truly life-changing. It has filled me with a sense of intimacy that my heart has always longed for. It causes me to go through my day with more joy in my heart and a smile on my face that never seems to leave. I'm less bothered by the criticisms of other people, I'm less aware of the condemnation that comes from the evil one, and I am more open to loving those who live and believe differently than I do. When I'm not lying in the lap of Christ on a daily basis, I'm grumpy, very cynical, painfully aware of my own insecurities, and all the more moved by the criticisms of others. Another way of putting it is that I'm simply living outside the light that Christ shines upon me. It doesn't mean that I've lost my salvation or that Christ loves me less than before; it simply means that I must become aware of my shortcomings, repent, and step back into the light of Christ that best guides me. This doesn't mean then that I (or we) become invincible to spiritual attacks or trials of various kinds. Jesus said very clearly that we would have difficult times in this life, but to take heart because He has overcome the world.

Since Jesus has overcome the world, this should be all the more the reason to rest our heads in His lap. Whatever has haunted you in the past or even the present is not anywhere near enough to keep Him from loving you. We only must humble ourselves. Once again, this is nothing we can do on our own. All we must do is lift our voices to Him and say as a blind man did in Luke 18:38, "Jesus, Son of David, have mercy on me!"

It doesn't get any more raw or true than this. Jesus is saying that you don't have to cut through red tape, go through loopholes, or do any sort of penance in order to enter His presence, to know Him, and ultimately make Him known.

## Question for Reflection

What is the "old man" in your life? Have you put it to sleep? Or does it still nip at your heels?

# 8
# His Great Pleasure

> "Your eyes saw my unformed body;
> all the days ordained for me were written in your book
> before one of them came to be.
> 17 How precious to me are your thoughts,[a] God!
> How vast is the sum of them!"
> Psalm 139:16-17

FOR THE PAST SEVERAL DAYS, each day, I have been reading the first chapter of Ephesians over and over again. I have read this book many times; however, I have come to believe that the Spirit of God can move as He pleases. This means that at any time, He can choose to illuminate something to us in the pages of Scripture that we did not see before. Because Scripture is essential to daily growth and intimacy in our daily lives with the Holy Father, Son, and Holy Spirit, I would love nothing more than to simply copy and paste the entire chapter of Ephesians 1 within the pages of this manuscript; however, I want to leave room for you to dust off your Bible and read it for yourself. What I will do, though, is insert what I have found to be the most enlightening and powerful:

Ephesians 1:4-8:

"Even before he made the world, God loved us and chose us in Christ to be holy and without fault in his eyes. God decided in advance to adopt us into his own family by bringing us to himself through Jesus Christ. This is what he wanted to do, and it gave him great pleasure. So we praise God for the glorious grace he has poured out on us who belong to his dear Son. He is so rich in kindness and grace that he purchased our freedom with the blood of his Son and forgave our sins. He has showered his kindness on us, along with all wisdom and understanding." Again, I have chosen the rendering of the New Living Translation.

There is just something about the wording that shoots off explosions of joy from deep inside me. No other translation that I have read carries the phrase, "This is what he wanted to do, and it gave him great pleasure." The NIV and ESV say, "according to his pleasure and will." I in no way want to discredit the work of the NIV or ESV; I am simply stating that I believe that there is something beautiful about how the New Living Translation words things, particularly in context. I am going to go out on a limb and say that Ephesians 1 is one of the single greatest passages in all of Scripture in that it speaks of the maddest love the world has ever known. I am trying to find the words to describe how beautiful and majestic Verses 4-8 actually are. I cannot fathom the idea that God the Father, before the creation of the world, chose someone like myself.

You can almost insert your own name, as though it reads, "For he chose (insert your name here) to be holy and blameless in his sight." How radical and out of this world that the God of the universe looks at you and me and says, "I chose you." It stops me in my tracks, and rightfully so; it should stop you in yours. Automatically, a host of reasons why the Father shouldn't have chosen us arises, but, regardless, I still can imagine the Father saying, "I chose you." The simple truth is that this is very easy to forget if we are not mindful about being reminded daily. I've long had the idea of writing on a wall simple reminders of God's truth, yet I think that one wall would be a giant reminder of the fact that it was the Father's pleasure to choose me.

The question arises, then, can we ever exhaust the Father's pleasure for us? We have concluded from previous chapters that that is not possible, but it is no fault to be reminded over and over and over again, for the consequences for not remembering are huge. For example, after I give in to my flesh's weakness, I am overcome with the idea that the Father is angry with me and wants nothing more than to cast me from His sight. But if we go back to the story of the prodigal son, we can see that casting his son from his presence was the furthest thing from His mind.

Bringing punishment and wrath upon his son was far from his mind as well. When guilt and shame arrive at our doorstep, we must remember two things: The first thing to remember is that the Father poured out the wrath that we humans deserve onto His only beloved Son on the cross (Romans 3:24-25). What a mad love this is, that the Father of the universe would give up His only beloved Son as a ransom for many (Mark 10:45). It always amazed me that the Father is so complete in Himself and in perfect community within the Trinity, yet He chooses to share the weighty love that makes up the Father, Son, and Holy Spirit.

The second truth that we must remember is that there is a vast difference between godly grief and worldly guilt. My friend Ryan helped me to better understand this. Worldly guilt condemns the soul, and godly grief brings life and repentance. Scripture tells us that it is God's kindness that leads us to repentance (Romans 2:4), so when your heart starts lying in the lies of, "You suck; you're trash; God made a mistake in calling you His own," these are all lies and do not lead anyone back to the heart of the Father. Lastly, it is important to know that the Father will never change His mind about you. It's not as though God says, "I've had enough," and then strips you of all the promises that He has made to you, His beloved child.

## Question for Reflection

Read Ephesians 1. Let it sink down into the depths of who you are. Do you feel his pleasure for you?

# 9
# When We Fade

"I have fought the good fight, I have finished the race, I have kept the faith."
2 Timothy 4:7

IN ONE OF THE LAST INTERVIEWS I watched with Brennan Manning (I believe it was in his home), his body was frail, as though all life was being sucked from him. His body sank into a chair that seemed to be many times bigger than his weakened frame. Even the shirt that he was wearing was one that his thin body swam in. The look in his eyes suggested that he knew his physical existence was ending, but there was also a shalom, a trust, and a confidence that he knew God was with him in perfect faithfulness. As he reclined comfortably in his chair, he mentioned that God had "a thing for him," as though to say that God was crazy and madly in love with him and never left his side even on his worst of days.

It truly moved me in my soul that he would trust in God's faithfulness so much because I know in my own heart how unfaithful I am to the Father. I know that I am still very young in my body, but I know there will be a day when, like Brennan, my body will fade, and I will breathe my last breath. Death is inevitable, but the kind of trust that Brennan had in the love and faithfulness of God is something I could only hope to have. There seem to be more moments of frustrations and shaking my fist at the sky than moments of joy, joy in knowing that God simply loves me, and letting that be enough for my soul.

Instead, I get cranky when I'm still single at thirty-two, or when I don't feel like I have people (friends in my life) who actually appreciate me and like me. Much of it could probably be my own fault, but there is still a great amount to be said about letting God love me and being convinced of it. This being true, I often wonder if anything else really matters in life. Loved ones and having a spouse and kids are all beautiful gifts in life, but do they even begin to compare to the mad love of God? No, they do not. I think what happens is that we let our eyes and minds become so enthralled by people, places, and things that the love of God because a subtle backdrop in our lives. What would happen if we truly believed that God loved us that madly and deeply? Our perceptions of ourselves and others would change drastically. I've had to tell myself consistently that God is as mad about me as He is the person who hurts and annoys me. I want people to see Christ in my life, my actions, and my speech. As I grow older, I want to be more gentle, joyful, and more in touch with the heart of God than I was in years prior.

This largely includes letting the Spirit replace the dark parts of myself with His love; in other words, complete surrender and utter identity transformation are required. Again, as Brennan Manning would say, define yourself radically by the love of God. At the end of time, I'm convinced that nothing else will matter. Not the amount of money I had in my bank account, my social status, who I married, how many kids I had, or how much or little I attended church. Nothing but what I made of the love of God for myself and for others.

In this moment, regardless of whether you find yourself in good health or slowly fading, know that the Father, Son, and Holy Spirit will be the most loyal subjects in your life. This love will change you from the inside out. As it relates to suffering, many in the Reformed community will hold to the phrase "don't waste your suffering." Of course, this seems bizarre and even cold for a Christian to say, but underneath all the buzz, they simply mean that we should cling all the more to the promises and faithfulness of God. Let us meditate on the words, "My God, why have you forsaken me?" Though Jesus Himself uttered these words while He hung upon the cross, let us not look past all that is happening in a single monumental moment in Jesus asking such a bold and heartfelt question to His Father; we must take to the depths of our hearts what is happening. The Father has turned His eyes from His beloved Son, in order that we, beloved sons and daughters, may not ever have to experience a lacking in the Lord's presence and mercy. After hearing this line of reasoning, we may cry out, "This is madness!" And yet how mad it is for God to give us the words of John 3:16: "For God so loved the world that he gave his one and only son, that whoever believes in him shall not perish but have eternal life" (NIV).

Can you feel the promise that the Father is graciously extending to the world, that if we stubborn and hard-headed humans would simply open our minds and hearts to the fact that this mad love that the Father might have for us very well might be true, we then are opening ourselves to a love that every honest person has wanted, a love that will stay with us in sickness and in health, in life, in death, and beyond?

A few mornings ago, I was reading through the Psalms and was suddenly awestruck by the words of Psalm 52:8: "But I am like an olive tree flourishing in the house of God; I trust in God's unfailing love forever and ever" (NIV). I find the image of the olive tree flourishing in the house of God crucial, and I believe that we should view ourselves in the same regard. Even though our bodies may slowly or quickly die out, our souls flourish with beauty because we know God's love for us. As I grow older, I imagine myself becoming more tender and compassionate and far less entrapped by anger, bitterness, and frustration.

Another way of putting it is, I want to be more and more like Jesus as my life progresses. I even imagine myself less and less enslaved by addictive habits. This is to say that the work of being more gentle, compassionate, and more Christlike doesn't have to wait until years from now, but it can start now in this moment. It starts with the bold and brave trust that the Father will be with me until the end. It begins with a radical surrender to the love of the Father.

## Question for Reflection

As we fade (or get older), do you see yourself becoming more like Christ? Why or why not?

# 10
# Becoming Less

> "He must become greater; I must become less."
> John 3:30

I RECENTLY FOUND MYSELF at the age of thirty-two, and I know what an old fart I'm becoming. I've never cared much about age, in the sense that I've always felt young by taking good care of my body and mind. The fact is, the older I get the less I think of myself and the more I think of other people. As I grow older, I find myself wanting less and wanting to give more. As you can probably imagine, the Scripture passage that comes to my mind is John 3:30: "He must increase, but I must decrease" (ESV). Some might take it as taking care of yourself less and taking care of others more. Or caring less about what happens in your own life and focusing more on God. Both have a degree of truth, but if we think about the average stay-at-home parent who bends over backwards to care for the needs of their children, sometimes they don't even get to shower, eat, or brush their teeth. Why? Because the needs of the children are greater and more important. Though this is a very particular context, often our wants will not outweigh those around us.

Yet, I'm going to go out on a limb here and say that I don't believe that God is saying that we should completely let ourselves go to waste because He matters more. I think that misses the point altogether. I believe what God is pointing to is that when we learn to take the attention off ourselves and put it on Him, the joy in our spirits becomes much more. Again, it's not simply because we matter less or that our needs don't have value. It's the fact that as humans we become so fixated on pleasing ourselves that nothing fills us up or settles us. What does fill and settle us is only the presence of our loving Lord and loving others. I'm afraid that some people who would come across John 3:30 might not have a healthy view of themselves, and as such, it would be easier for those people to assume that they already don't matter. So, they already have that area covered, yet those same people have not encountered the heart of the Gospel.

When we think less of ourselves in a destructive manner, as though to say, "My life is meaningless; it doesn't matter if I live or die," we fail to see how much the Father has loved us through the Son, Jesus Christ. Furthermore, the Father has given us the Holy Spirit, who is the Comforter and Wonderful Counselor who lives inside us (John 14:26). Knowing that God loves us so greatly in this way frees us to love others in the way that God has loved us. After all, we love because He first loved us (1 John 4:19).

## Question for Reflection

In what ways can you allow yourself to decrease so that God can increase?

# 11
# His Love Compels Us to Move

> "Therefore go and make disciples of all nations, baptizing them in the name of the Father and of the Son and of the Holy Spirit."
> Matthew 28:19

NOW THAT WE SEE that becoming less does not necessarily mean seeing or treating ourselves in a degrading manner and that becoming less allows us to be more enthralled by the love of God and more prone to want to love others, let us examine how the latter plays out. 2 Corinthians 1:3-5 says this: "Blessed be the God and Father of our Lord Jesus Christ, the Father of compassion and the God of all comfort, who comforts us in all our troubles so that we can comfort those in any trouble with the comfort we ourselves have received from God. For just as the sufferings of Christ overflow to us, so also through Christ our comfort overflows" (DBT). It seems only right that we examine two key parts of this section:

First, "the Father of compassion and the God of all comfort." Indeed, it can be difficult to view God as the Father of compassion and God of all comfort when you have faced many tribulations throughout a lifetime. One can easily see the amount of suffering that I have endured in my own life as well. I once did not believe that if there was a God, He was one of compassion and comfort. Rather, the perception that was in my mind was that He was cruel and longed to watch people suffer. However, the truth of the matter is that He (God, our heavenly Father) is not like that by any stretch. I believe the reality is that God allows suffering and various forms of hardship in our lives in order that some might ultimately be affectionately drawn to His presence.

The reason the word "some" was used above is that some yield their hearts to the mad love of God. In the book Concerning Death: a Practical Guide for the Living, the author is asked, "What's a good way to approach a bitter, angry person?" The author responds by saying, "Slowly, patiently and with respect. The first step is probably to hear them out several times, yet to keep coming back." What the author is saying is not only correct, but it also reflects the heart of our heavenly Abba as well. Scripture, in fact, tells us that God is slow to anger (patient) in Psalm 103:8, and if we go back to the story of the prodigal son, we see how the father stands and longingly waits outside for a trace of his son's presence. He isn't thinking, "Man, I am going to beat this kid when I see him next." No, we see again that he takes off running toward his son, wraps his arms around him, and kisses him over and over, despite how dirty he is. One final note on suffering is that many skeptics claim that God cannot be loving and compassionate while allowing suffering of any kind to exist. Not even a hangnail or a stubbed toe. Yet, some people who endure great hardship find a deep sense of understanding, hope, and clarity sometime after the suffering and hardship has taken place.

One story that comes to mind stems from the life of Gary Habermas, who is a world-renowned scholar on the resurrection of Jesus. He and his wife Debbie had four kids, but tragedy struck when his wife went in for some routine tests, and the doctor's fears of Debbie having cancer ultimately came true. He writes that the pain he felt when his best friend (his wife) died was the worst pain that he could experience. What allowed Gary to endure such a dark time in his life? The resurrection of Jesus. Garry writes about being in a skeptical mindset after his wife died; he even considered becoming a Buddhist, but it was in that time that he learned how deeply the resurrection applied to life. Not only does the physical resurrection show that he could soon see his wife again in eternity, but Jesus was now his great peace and shalom.

Second: Moving from Comfort to Comfort—Now that we have seen how God, our heavenly Father, comforts us with compassion, let us examine how our heavenly Father moves us from compassion to compassion. When the Lord first opened my heart to the revelation of His love, it sank deep inside my heart. I would wake up early with an automatic smile on my face, humming songs to myself as I made my bed. It could easily be described as a new romantic relationship, but no one else knew about it. A small pocket of people knew about my conversion to Christianity but wasn't sure what that meant, and neither was I. There came a time, though, after this love settled, that I now understood that I had to do something with the love and compassion that was overflowing from the inside out and outside in, not in the sense that I had to prove to God how much I loved Him so that He could love me more, but because I could no longer contain the love that was (and is) inside me. Very early on, I learned that the love of God can meet us in the darkest pockets of life.

The compassion that the Lord has covered me with has thus allowed me to love the "least of these." In my eyes, the compassion of the Lord far outweighs a person's past or present life. It doesn't matter if one has been an alcoholic for most of their life and can't seem to get it together; it doesn't matter if one has lived as a prostitute and feels that they are too dirty and filthy for God to love them. The compassion of God that overflows in us and through us must compel us to walk into the lives of others who feel unworthy and unclean and share the light that we have. The love and compassion of God are most effective when we get off the couch and throw aside the fear of sharing the Gospel. Sharing the good news encompasses the compassion and love of God. In the Gospel of Mark Chapter 15, Jesus commands His disciples to go into the world and make disciples.

An interesting fact about this is that the disciples of Jesus were very flawed and imperfect people. Yet the love and compassion of God spurred them on to go into the world and share it with people along the way, with the hope that others would join the fold. Maybe you have a nagging sense of the compassion of God in your life, but you feel shy, socially awkward, or feel afraid of being looked at as some kind of freak for your love for God. You might even feel like less of a person because others appear to be smarter than you, be it in areas of science or mathematics, but those areas, though they're of great value, do not answer or respond to our greatest love.

Blaise Pascal, though he was and is one of the world's greatest philosophers, found that philosophy was not the one thing to fulfill the greatest need of his body and mind. This need was what he called the fire of God. Obviously, he could not have meant it as a literal fire because that would have rendered him incapable of making such a pointed statement. Rather it must be understood as a metaphor. The fire of God, as Pascal calls it, has much to do with the compassion the above passage is speaking of. Being that the fire of God invaded the life of Blaise Pascal so deeply, being that he stood so close to the fire of God, it's hard for me to believe that he could keep quiet about it. My guess is that he probably had some conversations with people who were close to him in his circle. Furthermore, other people in his life who were well versed in philosophy probably thought he was crazy, but I don't think that after he came so close to the love and compassion of God that he cared what people thought. He probably was more concerned about the state and condition of those he loved. This is exactly what compassion does to the heart and mind of the beloved.

The compassion of God gives us a clearer lens through which we view existence and those around us. When we stand as close to the fire of God as Blaise Pascal did, we begin to see the purpose of life as something other than getting the most of what we can out of it, and we see that people are not a means to an end.

The fire of God causes me to see people as more than atoms, skin, and bone. It has caused me to see people differently when they die. The naturalist believes that when a person dies, they simply become a pile of bones, and that's all there is. While it's true that the human body does become a sack of bones, the Christian perspective believes that there is a soul that either goes on to be in perfect intimacy with God, or it goes and lives in eternal separation (Hell) from the mad love of the Father.

Within the pages of Scripture, there is a tension between the free will of human beings and the foreknowledge of the Father. The Psalms tell us that the Father chooses whom He brings near (Psalm 65:4). At face value, this may seem cold or malicious of God to choose who He lets into His house, but we do this every day in a number of ways. If you're a parent and your son or daughter wants to bring someone of romantic significance home, would you not look and discern to see if the significant other truly has the best intentions in mind for your son or daughter? Of course you would, and sometimes as parents (or as people who have lived longer), we can see the bigger picture, or we can sense something about a person that our children cannot.

In my own life, I can remember having a love interest for a girl while still in high school. My parents were kind enough to let her come over a few times to get to know her. I noticed after a while that my parents were not fond of her. Of course, in my young, naïve state of mind, I thought it was because they didn't want me to be happy, or worse yet, "no one was ever good enough for them." But what they saw was that this girl was taking advantage of my kindness and tender disposition. It took a good deal of time to see that my parents were right; they saw the bigger picture. And had I ended up dating this girl long term; it would have ended up much worse. Overall, we as people generally lock our doors at night; why? To keep unwanted evil people from coming into our homes. It makes sense, then, that God would choose whom He would allow to come into His kingdom and even into the lives of His children.

He sees the bigger picture; He can see more deeply and widely than we ever could with human might. The father can see that in the heart of a person, that deep down in the pit of a person, they want nothing to do with the Father's purposes or will, and as such He says, "Thy will be done." Going a step further, simply because God knows the will and wants of every person, it does not mean that we are to keep the mad love of the Father to ourselves. Rather, we are to do as Jesus commanded the disciples to do in the Great Commission. It should be comforting that only the Father knows the outcome; it should fill us with hope and expectation because there is still time for people to come into close contact with the mad love that the Father has for them.

## Question for Reflection

**As a Christian, have you ever wanted to go comfort someone, but didn't because you were too afraid?**

# 12

## My Unfaithfulness and His Faithfulness

"What shall we say, then? Shall we go on sinning so that grace may increase? By no means! We are those who have died to sin; how can we live in it any longer?"

Romans 6:1-2

IT OCCURRED TO ME this morning as I was cleaning up around my bedroom/office, the level of my unfaithfulness to the Father. It hit me like I had taken a punch in the stomach. Then, I could instantly feel waves of condemnation invading my mind and my insides, and for a second, I thought that maybe I deserved to feel this feeling of shame and guilt. But then I recalled, once again, my favorite words of Romans 8:1-2:

"There is therefore now no condemnation for those who are in Christ Jesus. For the law of the spirit of life has set you free in Christ Jesus from the law of sin and death" (ESV). These words allowed for room in my soul; they allowed me to work my way through what was going on inside me. I quickly realized that what I was experiencing was not God's anger toward me, but His love toward me. I also realized that, despite my unfaithfulness in walking in His ways, He was still there in my moments of weakness to hear my cry of repentance. This, then, is not a green light to go out and live any way we please, but to embrace and live in the grace that the Father has for us.

Timothy Keller says, "Men, you'll never be a good groom to your wife unless you're first a good bride to Jesus." Getting married one day is one of the biggest desires of my heart, and yet one of the biggest obstacles that get in the way of that is my own addiction to

## My Unfaithfulness and His Faithfulness

lust. Sobriety has been a tough undertaking, every day choosing to fight back against desires that I know will not bring me into deeper intimacy with God or closer to meeting a woman with whom I could be in a relationship and one day call my wife. For that to happen, there needs to be a heart that has a bent toward faithfulness and toward a future. In the same way, there needs to be that same faithfulness in my friendship with Jesus. In Matthew's Gospel, Jesus says, "These people honor me with their lips, but their hearts are far from me." (15:8, NIV) It is one thing to say that you love God, or that He means everything to you, but if your actions don't back it up, it's all lip service. Is it possible, then, for any human being to live a fully consistent life? No, but when it comes to our love for significant others and our love for God, there must be consistency.

When it comes to relationships that have intimacy and trust is violated, it can be very hard to trust again. Sometimes those who have experienced this hurt may forgive but feel that they cannot extend their souls to the person in the same way again; thus, a boundary is established to wisely guard themselves against further trauma. Other times, people have the deepest struggle to forgive and only want the offender to vanish from their lives (sometimes rightfully so). Yet the faithfulness of God is something different than we ever could have imagined. For the one who places themselves firmly in the love of God, the Father tenderly inks upon our hearts, "I will never leave you nor forsake you." Even further, the book of Romans speaks to us the following words:

"For those whom he foreknew he also predestined to be conformed to the image of his Son, in order that the Son might be the firstborn among many brothers" (Romans 8:29, ESV). Here we see that even before the foundation of the world, God saw you and said, "You're mine." This is not a pathway to stroke our human egos, but rather to realize that God saw us in all our filth and unfaithful hearts and affectionately called us to Himself. This, in many ways, should bring us to our knees in humility because we as humans do not deserve this kind of mad love and grace. Rather, it seems even more fitting that we deserve the consequences of our unfaithfulness and bad actions. Along with this sobering humility, we should also recite these words to our souls daily, that while we were still sinners, Christ died for us (Romans 5:8). While you, me, and everybody else is helplessly enslaved to our own selfish compulsions, Christ died for us; why? Because He knew that there would be no other way for us to be free of our bondage to ourselves. Now because we have this mad and faithful love, it does not mean that we can continue to live carelessly, or that there won't be consequences (past, present, or future), but with God's mad love and faithfulness, we can face anything with a resilient spirit. If you find that, at this moment in time, you're losing everything, know that Jesus gave you everything because of His death, burial, and resurrection. The faithfulness of God will disarm you and arm you at the same time. What I mean is, first, that God's faithfulness strips us of our pride.

While some hold to pride being a good thing, yet our pride is what can prevent us from changing in the deepest of ways. Take, for example, someone who has lived a life of addiction their entire life. Those around them may know full well that there is a huge problem in play, but to them everything is fine. When confronted on the matter, they will keep insisting that they don't have a problem. Going a step further, they might even get angry when confronted about the issue. But why? Because you're trying to expose or remove something from them, and pride implies, "I don't have a problem." Humility implies, "Yes, I have a problem, and by God's grace I will do everything I can to wage war against it."

The faithfulness of God empowers us in this way, to confess and admit that we have a problem in our lives that needs to be resolved. Why? Because we know that He will not leave our side. Notice again that God's faithfulness does not mean that there will not be earthly consequences. However, consequences are not something to ultimately fret about.

Though they may be troubling in the beginning, or maybe for quite some time, they are not outside of God's authority and redemption. This also means that God can bring new life and restoration to even the darkest situations that are without hope. I have learned that, as Christians, we must wear His faithfulness as a soldier wears armor. If we do not, we are open to a world of attacks, and the enemy that we face knows how to attack us in various ways, yet we must be in touch with ourselves enough to understand what those areas are that the enemy looks to exploit. If we don't, we will be devoured before we can even begin to put up a fight.

For me, those areas of attack are anger and self-loathing, both of which are areas of my life that I am often disgusted with. And most times I am ambushed before I realize that I'm in a fight. Anger comes to the forefront of my life, and I forget His faithfulness like someone who forgets to take their medication. Often, I'm angered by the fact that something in my life isn't going as planned, or that things are not going per my time frame. I often act like someone completely different when the anger has its way, and I hate this about myself. I completely forget about who I am and who God is. Along with the anger comes heaviness of the soul and depression, followed by thoughts that my life should end and tears that serve to let the anguish out.

It's in these moments that I hear a voice say: "Brandon, I love you, I am here, and it is going to be okay." Knowing that I have just confessed to hearing a voice, it would be easy for some to cast me off as having a mental disorder, but I think it's a lot different when the voice one hears brings calm to your soul. It's different when this voice turns anger into peace when this voice turns self-loathing into healthy self-love and liking for myself. The voice that says, "I love you," is the only voice that can speak overall paralyzing fears and insecurities that we might find in ourselves. The more I let this voice speak over my life, the more it doesn't matter what others think of me or the reputation that precedes me because it only matters what He thinks of me.

## Question for Reflection

Are you as faithful to God as you should be? In what areas of your life can you be doing better?

# 13
# My Greatest Reward

> "I press on toward the goal to win the prize for which God has called me heavenward in Christ Jesus."
> Philippians 3:14

IF YOU HAVE EVER been struck by the feeling that you have wasted your life or thrown it away due to various life choices, fret not because you're in great company. Many times in my life have I felt this way; even going back to college in my late twenties and finishing in my early thirties has been something that has made me question myself and even God at times. I can remember early on in my freshman year of college wondering if I was even cut out for college; there was some adjustment anxiety ongoing in my life. When the desire to go back to school was born again inside me, I argued for what seemed to be an eternity with my mom about moving out of the house and onto a college campus. Of course, she didn't like it at first, but when she saw that I could function on my own as an adult, the tide changed.

Even as I spent the first few days on campus, I still felt the effects of a huge culture shock—the shock of not knowing anyone, the shock of what seemed to be a lot of academic work, and the shock of being somewhat socially reserved and somewhat awkward. I would sit in my dorm during the first days and sob. I didn't know what the following years of my life would look like, and I wrestled with myself because of not having taken things more seriously. I hated the fact that I could have finished these parts of my life sooner. Before I knew it, I was emailing my advisor and scheduling a meeting to speak with him. When I met with him early on a Friday, I believe the first words out of my mouth were, "I don't know if I can do this; I don't know if I'm supposed to be here." That was, at least, my way of trying to sound spiritual or trying to believe that God didn't want me at this small college. Thankfully, my advisor kindly suggested that I give it more time, and if I still wasn't happy with where I was, he would gladly assist me in getting out the same way I had entered. I would love to say that everything was bright and wonderful from that point on, but the same feeling that haunted me at the beginning of my college career would haunt me continually as the months and years progressed. It wasn't merely education and academics that I felt had been completely squandered in my life, but it was everything else that was associated with a prosperous life.

Not only am I, at the age of thirty-two, just graduating college, but I am considering my first real job. And while it might be easy to say, "Better late than never," something inside me cannot help but feel as though I have gotten behind in the race we call life. I don't believe that life is a race, but that maybe we are conditioned to believe that if we have most things done by a certain time in life, everything runs more smoothly—if we have a decent-paying job, maybe we're married and have kids with an awesome house of our own. I'll gladly grant that there is some truth to the fact that maybe if we had done certain things differently in our lives things might have ended up differently, yet we are here now, and we can't change what happened earlier on in life. Maybe, like me, you find yourself behind in the so-called race of life. The first bit of hope and even comfort that can be provided is that we first must throw aside the weighted belief that life is a race and replace it with the understanding that God is in control and that we must fix our thoughts on things above.

First, if God is in control of everything in our lives, then we don't have to race for anything, meaning that we don't have to compete against anybody for anything in life. So what if it takes you or me longer to accomplish something in life? It shouldn't take away from our value or worth as humans; instead, there should be a trust that God is moving and working for our good. I say "should" for the simple fact that trusting God at times can be extremely difficult because we cannot see what's ahead waiting for us. When we can't see what is in front of us, it's easy to become angry and frustrated and think that the Father doesn't have our best interest in mind or that His love isn't as mad as we think.

I have come to believe that the Father controls everything in my life and your life, down to the tiniest specs of our existence, even all the mistakes and horrible things that have taken place. I realize that this statement might come as shocking and might rally up emotions that stem from not having mass amounts of free will. But the fact is that the Father has used every single dark and gloomy moment of my life for my good. Again, we might not see it as our good right now, but that does not mean that goodwill not be discovered later. The greatest examples are one: martial arts have always been my first love; they were something that my father raised me in. I was actively engaged in them until I was seventeen or eighteen. I was even helping my father teach youth and some adult classes at both of his schools. As time went on, though, my dad got very sick and was enduring some other personal hardships and sadly had to close the school that he was running. Both my dad and I did not touch martial arts after that point. As the schools shut down, I discovered that regenerating faith that I now have, and martial arts and teaching were the furthest things from my heart.

The desires of my heart were all about God and ministry, and with that, I went through a year-long Bible program. At the time I felt that there was a "call from God" to full-time ministry, or at least to working in a church setting, but it didn't work out that way. I wanted to be a youth pastor, but there wasn't a shred of opportunity for me. At that point was when I started writing my first book, and all you must do is read it to know all the details of what went into it. The point is, God set aside my love for martial arts so that I could then start working on my writing career, and, along with my writing, I also began to embark on motivational speaking, sharing my own story and how the mad love of the Father has not only saved but changed my life. And though these avenues are not very lucrative yet, I'm doing them and using them as a means of ministry and honoring God with my gifts. Doing these things without much outward success has been a joy, though there have been times where I have lusted after the success of others, but I have realized that Jesus is my ultimate, most pure, and truest reward—the only reward that truly matters in this lifetime, the only reward that we Christians should be concerned about, in honesty.

This morning, I was once again reflecting on the story of the prodigal son; however, this time my attention was fixed upon the older brother and how he reacted to how the Father responded to the younger brother. The younger brother was a spoiled, stuck-up brat, who wanted the inheritance that his father had for him, and who in turn went and blew all his money and found himself eating pig slop. He returned home and had a grand speech in mind, but the mad love that the father had for the younger son compelled him to sprint toward the son, which in that time was unheard of for a father to do. But the father sprints towards his younger son and wraps his arms around him and kisses him repeatedly. The older son, then, I can imagine walking out the front door of their home and seeing his father lovingly embracing his younger brother.

The father then decides to throw a party, but the older brother refuses to go in. This is how the conversation between the older son and the father goes:

"But he answered his father, 'Look! All these years I've been slaving for you and never disobeyed your orders. Yet you never gave me even a young goat so I could celebrate with my friends. But when this son of yours who has squandered your property with prostitutes comes home, you kill the fattened calf for him!'

"'My son,' the father said, 'you are always with me, and everything I have is yours. But we had to celebrate and be glad because this brother of yours was dead and is alive again; he was lost and is found'" (Luke 15:29-32, NIV)

Two things that stick out in the father's response to the older brother are: 1) He has always been with the older. This could easily be another way for the father to say, I will never leave you nor forsake you. Which asks the question, why isn't the Father's presence enough for us? Consider the lyrics to the amazing hymn "Come Thou Fount":

Oh, to grace how great a debtor

daily I'm constrained to be!

Let thy goodness, like a fetter,

bind my wandering heart to thee:

Prone to wander, Lord, I feel it,

prone to leave the God I love;

Here's my heart, O take and seal it;

seal it for thy courts above.

The older son, though he did not physically run away from home, let his heart run away. He forgot who he belonged to and how good he had it. Then he began to envy the younger brother for the reception he was receiving from the father and how the father was treating the younger. It was as though he said within himself, "I never got that royal kind of treatment!" In some way, all humans do that. And, while it doesn't make it any more right, I believe it only proves that we can never be satisfied unless we know who the ultimate source of satisfaction is. Saint Augustine penned the classic words, "Our heart is restless until it rests in you," and his words hit with such accuracy on the human condition. It's easy to get caught up in the affairs of this world, be it the amount of money in our bank account or even the amount of praise and accolades. It's true in my own life that even if I had over a million dollars in my bank account, I would probably be happy and content for a brief time before I wanted more. The same can be said of praise and accolades. My work could be praised by millions, but it wouldn't be long until one negative comment deflated my ego, or I began to feel like I wasn't seen by others.

Considering the Christian eternity with the Father and His mad love for us, what does any earthly pursuit matter? Let us also consider the words from Paul in Philippians 3:7-11 "But whatever were gains to me I now consider loss for the sake of Christ. 8 What is more, I consider everything a loss because of the surpassing worth of knowing Christ Jesus my Lord, for whose sake I have lost all things. I consider them garbage, that I may gain Christ and be found in him, not having a righteousness of my own that comes from the law, but that which is through faith in Christ – the righteousness that comes from God on the basis of faith. I want to know Christ—yes, to know the power of his resurrection and participation in his sufferings, becoming like him in his death, and so, somehow, attaining to the resurrection from the dead" (NIV).

In short, Paul is saying, I just want Him, for He is my greatest reward. All the older son could see was how the celebration was of epic proportions, and how he wanted the very treatment that his younger brother got. His perspective, his view of things, was blinded by earthly things that will ultimately fade.

Scripture tells us that Heaven throws a party for one sinner who repents (Luke 15:7). The father used what was in his means to throw the younger brother a party but only try and imagine what the rejoicing and celebration in Heaven are like when a prodigal son or daughter returns home. The celebration that the father put on for his younger son would pale in comparison to the amount of celebration and rejoicing that would take place. Scripture also tells us to set our sights on things above

(Colossians 3:2); furthermore, Scripture tells us in 2 Timothy 2:3-4 "Join me in suffering, like a good soldier of Christ Jesus. A soldier refrains from entangling himself in civilian affairs, in order to please the one who enlisted him" (NIV).

It would be simple to think after reading the above text that we aren't supposed to care or have any feeling or emotion toward anything and should live a life of detachment, as some worldviews would say, but that would fly in the face of the character of Jesus; He wept and showed emotions over various things. The only difference was that He knew who His ultimate allegiance was to and where His ultimate residence was. In the same way, we should learn to live a life with one foot raised toward Heaven and one foot here on earth. Like Jesus, and like David the psalmist, we will experience great joys and hardships. Yet it is very critical that we constantly are reminding ourselves that the joy we experience in this life is nothing compared to the joy that He will give, and the hardships we face are nothing to compared to the joy and healing that we are going to receive in His presence, for He is our greatest reward.

## Question for Reflection

Can you say that Christ is the greatest reward of your life? If not, what have you treasured more than him? Also, what regrets in your life can you give over to God?

# 14
# You Were Such a ...

> "Finally, all of you, have unity of mind, sympathy, brotherly love, a tender heart, and a humble mind."
> 1 Peter 3:8

THE OLDER I GET, the more sensitive my heart becomes. I know that that is not typical of most men to say, but it is true for me. You could even say that the older I get, the more I am embracing the more sensitive side of myself. Despite my love for teaching self-defense and watching combat sports, I still see myself as a sensitive guy. There is a recent psychological study that covers what is now known as Highly Sensitive People. This study was founded by Dr. Elaine Aron, and my own investigation of this topic began over a year ago, which was when I began to realize that I no longer wanted to live with a tough guy façade. As I said before, I love martial arts and teaching, but for me, that is less about leading a violent lifestyle and more a means to help others have the confidence to protect themselves and loved ones, thus leading a more peaceful life. But even with that, I began to also notice how I reacted to the environment around me. It could be the emotions of others or the sensation between people, but these areas of life went far beyond introversion and empathy.

When I begin to feel the energy from people, especially negative energy, it's very draining to my entire being. Not only do I feel physically tired, but I feel tired emotionally, mentally, and spiritually as well, almost like Elijah in 1 Kings 19, when he runs away and begs for God to take his life. Not in the sense that I am suicidal, but that what I am feeling is very overwhelming in a myriad of ways, and being in the arms of the Father (in eternity) sounds appealing. Again, I know how weird this sounds, and I have wrestled against this part of myself for the longest time. I have seen the sensitive side of myself as more of a hindrance than a blessing. I have tried to be tougher and not let things in life stick to me so deeply, but I think that it can be a huge blessing (and an act of grace) to be a sensitive person. Sometimes Christians speak of being sensitive to the Spirit. I think that when a person has the qualities of a highly sensitive person, the sensitivity to the Spirit comes as almost a given, while others must almost become aware or keen to it. Not saying that highly sensitive people don't need work in the area, but it is almost like a heightened sense that God has put in us, that even we can't suppress.

Lately, I have been dwelling on two instances in my youth; one is a memory of a classmate my senior year of high school, when they wrote on the back of a senior picture, "You were such a ******," and they were right because at that time my heart was like that of a stone; and another time when I was a kid, a fellow classmate that I had grown up with said, "You were such a jerk." She, too, was right because, at that time, I was a bully with my wheelchair who ran over people's feet. Perhaps the Father is working in my sensitive self as a way for me to realize that I don't want to be the ****** with the cold and hard heart or the person who is violent because he can be. As much as being a highly sensitive person drives me crazy at times, I have come to believe that is one of the things that God likes about me and that it doesn't take away from His mad love for me. I will say this plainly, it's okay to be a highly sensitive person, though I also believe it is wise to learn how to protect and care for our sensitive self. It is okay, and the person who is sensitive is not sinning by being that way. In other words, your sensitivity and mine are not a means by which the Father is punishing us.

In Christ, sensitivity is a gift that can be used to bring us into His presence. As mentioned before, having a natural sense of sensitivity to the Holy Spirit opens the soul of a person, and this seems to be natural and yet intensified. As a highly sensitive person myself, the more I truly began to be in touch with this gift, the more heavily and more boldly I felt and sensed the conviction of the Spirit. Though the conviction is heavy, it is not out of anger but kindness (Romans 2:3-4). Again, I am not saying that highly sensitive people feel the conviction of God more than non-sensitive people, but that to a non-sensitive person the conviction of the Spirit can feel like a dull pain. Regardless of how one might react to the conviction of the Spirit, it can be very easy to run away from it, much like Jonah did. When I experience the conviction of God, I fail to see it as kindness. I fail to see it as kindness because I know that I willingly choose to live outside of God's mad love for me. But even though I stray, my spirit is deeply aware of His mad love calling me to come back into His arms.

The mad love of God, to me, is like that of a lover whose heart aches for their beloved to come to them. For many highly sensitive people, they can feel like social outcasts and not have a place to call home, which is why highly sensitive people find shelter in the arms of the Father, for you are no outcast to Him; He knows every single hair on your head. He knows every desire and thought that comes your way. I am in no way saying that highly sensitive people have an easier path to God. The need for faith and repentance granted by the Holy Spirit is a must. No one ever gets to bypass the gatekeeper. What I am saying is that God has a soft spot for highly sensitive people.

Being that I am a highly sensitive person, and being that I feel emotions very deeply, it can be rather difficult to approach the Father. As such, I truly must remember that His love for me never changes, that He never simply loves and adores me one day and loathes me the next.

The Father's disposition is not changing as my own, where I am happy one moment and despairing of life the next. Rather, His love is always constant, and once again we must dwell on the fact that if we are in Christ, nothing can separate us from the love of God. Therefore, we must learn to weigh the various thoughts and emotions that we allow to come into us. Some days my own thoughts and heart condemn me:

You're not good enough

You'll never measure up

You're a disgrace

God hates you

No one loves you

You name it, the lies have made their way into the chambers of my soul. Often, they stay there locked away in their own separate areas, and sometimes I don't know those lies are still taking up residence. The only way that I know how to deal with these lies is through the light of the Gospel. 1 John 3:19-20 says: "This is how we know that we belong to the truth and how we set our hearts at rest in his presence: if our hearts condemn us, we know that God is greater than our hearts, and he knows everything" (NIV). Furthermore, we must learn to take every thought captive, as we are told in 2 Corinthians 10:5. This acts as a shield for the sensitive soul from self-condemnation and hate. Learning to accept that God gave you sensitivity as a gift can be very difficult, and there will always be times where you are different. But your gift of sensitivity is just what humanity may need.

Being able to shed tears with someone can sometimes create the greatest bonds between people; after all, Jesus shed many tears both on the cross and in the Garden of Gethsemane (John 11). Moving ahead to Verse 32, Martha says to Jesus, "Lord, if you had been here, my brother would not have died." Martha not only strikes me as a sensitive person but someone who is prone to state what she sees as obvious. In Luke 10, there is a scene where Jesus is visiting Mary and Martha in their home. Mary is content to be at the feet of Jesus, as everyone should be. But Martha has a restless soul that can only see the work that needs to be done around her. I'd assume that, much like myself, she begins to feel very panicky and anxious on the inside. Maybe her chest tightens up, maybe it begins to be difficult for her to breathe, and maybe, like me, she feels on the verge of tears. I believe that in this experience and in the death of her brother, Jesus knew and felt her pain in a way nobody else could. Jesus felt the pain on a cosmic level. More so, I believe that He felt the weight of sin and its consequences, and He ultimately knew that He would be on the receiving end of those consequences when it came to the cross.

Because Jesus felt so deeply in this way, the highly sensitive person should be willing to approach the presence of Christ with confidence, trust, and hope, for the very reason that the highly sensitive person is loved far beyond their wildest expectations and because the Father has your ultimate good in mind. Once again, it can be hard to believe that in the mad love of the Father is our greatest good, especially when we can feel a world of different emotions and hurts, but Christ does not leave us to the weight of the various hurts and emotions that we can feel daily. In this way, the following two aids that the Father graciously provides us are methods to help us in our thinking that being highly sensitive is not a punishment but a blessing.

The first aid that the Father gives us is that He is close to the brokenhearted (Psalm 34:18). Many times, as a highly sensitive person, it can feel as though you are going through life with a permanently broken and wounded heart, and it feels like no one can empathize or understand. Yet the psalmist David emphatically tells us that the Lord Jesus is close to us, closer than we may allow ourselves to believe. Proverbs 18:24 tells us that Jesus is not only our friend but that He is closer than a brother. This truth cannot be a mere cognitive belief but must be a belief that encompasses all that we are. When this happens, we can find a spirit of hope, resilience, and healing. The second aid that our Lord provides is the ability to cast our cares on Him (1 Peter 5:7) Why? Because He cares for us. Thus, when we feel overwhelmed by sorrow and hurt, rather than running away from the presence of the Father, we can confidently approach Him, and He will gladly take from us the burdens that we cast at His feet. Tying this all together, we will see that for the highly sensitive person when they arrive at the understanding that our Lord is closer than we believe and that we can depend on Him, they can access their deepest and fullest form of happiness in who their King is and who they are.

## Question for Reflection

Would you consider yourself to be a sensitive person? How can we then use Ephesians 6 to guard ourselves? If you are not a very sensitive person, how then might you be more mindful of your actions to others who might be?

# 15
# A Constant Smile

> "Those who look to him are radiant;
> their faces are never covered with shame."
> Psalm 34:5

EVER SINCE I WAS A KID, there was a smile on my face, no matter what was going on. Even as an adult, people compliment me on my smile and how it is almost always there. Though there have been many times of tears and seasons of sadness in my life, the constant smile that God gave me would breakthrough as the sun breaks through the clouds. Yes, I truly believe He gave me the smile as a gift and a reminder of where He has brought me from and where He is taking me. The Bible speaks a lot about joy—over two hundred times, in fact—enough for anyone to understand that God is serious about our joy. Yet, there has been a long struggle for me as it pertains to the topic of joy. Even though there is often a smile on my face, there is often a struggle going on below the surface. Despite that, it has always been easy to make me smile, no matter how hard I try not to. When I was completing my undergraduate degree, my friend Jesse could always see when I wasn't smiling, and as such he would go out of his way to make me smile, which, to be honest, kind of annoyed me at times because I didn't want to smile.

I would have much rather dwelt upon what was weighing me down on the inside, but I believe that the reason that he wanted me to smile so much was that he wanted me to remember hope, or rather the hope that God has given. But what do things like hope and joy naturally look like for different people? For some, hope and joy might seem to be a spiritual elation so to speak, where people are so high on Jesus that things such as depression or anxiety never exist. And this has always troubled me because if one has followed any amount of my writing, it's plain to see that anxiety and depression have been antagonists in my life. As such, my walk with God has not resembled that of a charismatic or prosperity preacher.

But does joy always look that way? And is it possible for those who live with anxiety and depression to have joy even despite such peril? The other day I was reading through a small booklet on grief, and the author (Brent Curtis) had this to say about joy: "Joy doesn't necessarily feel good. But it's always hopeful. And it creates a focus on reality beyond oneself." The words of Brent Curtis helped me immensely; on one hand, there wasn't a sense of condemnation in my soul because it freed me from having to be like the slap-happy Christians that surrounded me most of the time at college. I don't have anything against them, but the fact is that over time I grew very tired of having to pretend to be happy and act like I wasn't in any type of physical or psychological pain. Even with the pain, there was something inside me that clung to the heart of Christ. And even though there was (or is) pain in my life, my hope is still deeply rooted in Christ. Joni Eareckson Tada has always been a huge source of inspiration for me, a woman who in my opinion has done more to improve the lives of others from her wheelchair than when she was an able-bodied person. Joni is a quadriplegic, who was going to take a fun leap into the Chesapeake Bay when she misjudged the shallowness of the water. As a result, Joni ended up with a fracture between the fourth and fifth cervical. Before her accident, Joni had enjoyed several different sports and pastimes. One can only imagine the amount of anger, frustration, despair, and depression that she experienced in the beginning and throughout her journey.

Lord knows it has been much of the same in my own life, thinking that you'll never be able to amount to much with the condition of your being. For Joni, her situation was a trifecta; not only was her body affected, but her mind and spirit as well. Not only would she need to be reminded of God's truth and love, but her mind and spirit would need love and care. The road to healing for Joni would be long and tortuous, with many more hardships along the way. The point is that, with time, Joni began (by God's grace) to find her grounding again in God's love, and she began to find her smile again. Joni then would become an advocate for the disabled community, a bestselling author, artist, and singer. She is a testimony to what the mad love of God can do even in the worst of situations.

I've always found comfort in the fact that Jesus was a man of sorrows; it never occurred to me that God-Jesus might have smiled, too. I say might because there is no clear-cut evidence in Scripture, though we do have the book of Ecclesiastes, which tells us that there is a time for everything (Ecclesiastes 3), and if Jesus was God in the flesh (fully human) would that not then mean that He had a sense of humor as well? Wouldn't that mean that He smiles and laughs similarly to how we finite humans do, even though the humor of Jesus is not crude as our human attempts at humor can be? I believe that the fact remains that if He was human like us and experienced anger and sadness like us, it only makes sense that He smiled and laughed as well. Furthermore, in Matthew 19:14, Jesus commands that the little children come to Him without hindrance. Obviously, there was something about Jesus that drew children to Him, and in some religious artwork, we see Jesus joyfully embracing them. If this is the case, it would be quite simple to imagine the children smiling at Jesus and Jesus smiling back at them.

I can remember the first time the Holy Spirit invaded my life. I simply could not stop smiling, for such peace had entered me. Another time that I experienced something very similar was when I was at a retreat and the guest speaker came over to me after he was done with his sermon and asked if he could pray for my healing. Now, I know that this can be a very touchy subject, especially for those of us who live with cerebral palsy or other conditions. But, as the speaker came over to me, he gently placed his hands on my head and began to pray for my healing. And as he did that, others began to gather around me. I don't remember it being any crazy spectacle like one would see on television, where a faith healer touches someone and they either fall or go flying backwards. It was more an act of love; while the people prayed for my healing, some prayed for the healing of cerebral palsy from my body, which I took no offense to because I knew that there was a deeper purpose for my having this condition. Yet, through the moments of prayer, I could beyond a shadow of a doubt know that my heart and soul were being healed by the mad love of God, which in my estimation is far more important than physical healing for anyone who professes faith in Christ. During the prayer session, a constant smile was on my face. Do I believe that the Father was smiling as well? Yes, I do. I wonder how much Christianity would change if people understood that God wasn't waiting to devour them. My intention is to simply state that if the only understanding people have of the Father is an angry being holding a lightning bolt in His hand, they will never come to Him in faith and repentance. Think of a child who has a parent with a constant temperament of anger; do you think that they will naturally come to them with joy and expectation? No, they would much more likely act in a fearful and timid manner, not knowing when the parent will have another outburst. Again, I am not suggesting that the Father is not capable of anger and unleashing justice, for it is grossly incoherent to believe that a God of love would not possess in Himself the ability to defend the cause of His people.

But how does one begin to wear this seemingly divine smile? A pastor once said that the good news is bad news first, which, when it comes down to it, means that you and I are not the good people that we make ourselves out to be. This leads us to embrace total honesty about ourselves, which then leads us out of darkness and into a great light. It leads us to the way of trust.

## Question for Reflection

Do you believe that God smiles at you? Or do you believe that he is constantly angry with you?

# 16
# A Divine Trust

> "It's amazing what we can do if we will trust God enough to step out of our comfort zones!"
> Brett Harris, *Do Hard Things*

TRUST IS A DIFFICULT undertaking for many reasons. Perhaps you trust too easily, and, as a result, your heart is wounded and penetrated far too easily, which then creates the feeling and perception of not wanting to love ever again. I've been there myself, many a time. But this perception is a momentary safeguard from the pain that was caused for us. Eventually, that safeguard wears off, and we find ourselves on the quest for love and fulfillment again. Sadly, I've just described the human condition as it relates to us as broken people. Somehow, we start to believe that one person or one moment in life can fill and heal us in the way that our souls long for most. But experience should tell us that this is not the case. The same can be said as it relates to trust in God. And what I have realized (for me, anyway) is that my trust and faith in God is an uneven flow where, for a moment or season, I trust God in a passionate and unrelenting way, but in the next moment, when something bad happens, I fail to trust Him altogether.

What is most frustrating is that the Lord has never given me a reason to doubt and not trust. He has always provided and come through me for me in all circumstances. Rather, the doubt and inability to trust Him comes from my lack of belief, the applicable passage being Mark 9, where a father brings his son to Jesus. The man is begging Jesus to heal his son if Jesus is willing, and Jesus replies, "willing, all things are possible for those who believe." And, as Christians know and often exclaim, the father answers, "I believe, but help my unbelief." I think that this passage is often quoted because it speaks so plainly to our own condition.

We feel the divide between our want to believe and all the lingering fears, questions, and desires that remain. Some days I don't believe at all, it seems, or I feel that I am functioning as an agnostic. But then I feel the Spirit drawing me to repent and rest in intimacy in the mad love of the Father. A second Scripture passage that comes to mind is Matthew 14, when Peter walks on water. Apart from those who will scoff at the idea of whether a human being can actually walk on water, I'd like to focus on the bigger and deeper picture.

It almost seems that something moves or shifts inside Peter when he sees Jesus, yet at first, he and the other disciples think Jesus is a ghost. In our own time, we would have thought that seeing Jesus was an illusion or some sort of special effect. Peter's response is not much different from doubting Thomas's; both of them demanded a sign of reassurance. Thomas wanted to touch the body of Christ, and Peter wanted to come near Christ if it was truly Him. I liken Peter's falling into the water to trying to walk on my own as a kid; I got all excited and took my focus off what I was doing for a split second, and bam, I was on the floor. The moral of the story, in a faith sense, is that when we take our eyes off Christ for a second and notice our circumstances, we sink into the deep of ourselves.

In these moments, we see our frailty and how quick to desert Christ we are. My inner disposition goes from an optimist to a pessimist. I start telling myself that nothing will improve in my life and that I am merely a product of my circumstances. Yet Christ still calls on us to trust Him. He calls us to not fixate on prior circumstances but to only focus on Him. He calls us to have a divine faith, a faith that only that the promised Holy Spirit can produce in us. It should be clear, though, that simply because the Spirit produces new life and desires in us, it doesn't guarantee that we will win the war between spirit and flesh (Galatians 5:17).

For that matter, one might feel as though they have little to no victory over their fleshly desires. But, our feelings cannot and must not be a baseline for how the Lord feels about us or how we feel God feels about us. On any given day, regardless of how I feel or don't feel, I remind myself of Ephesians 2:1-7: "And you were dead in the trespasses and sins in which you once walked, following the course of this world, following the prince of the power of the air, the spirit that is now at work in the sons of disobedience— among whom we all once lived in the passions of our flesh, carrying out the desires of the body and the mind, and were by nature children of wrath, like the rest of mankind. But God, being rich in mercy because of the great love with which he loved us, even when we were dead in our trespasses, made us alive together with Christ—by grace you have been saved—and raised us up with him and seated us with him in the heavenly places in Christ Jesus, so that in the coming ages he might show the immeasurable riches of his grace in kindness toward us in Christ Jesus" (ESV).

One may ask, how can I know God truly loves me? Or, another way of putting it is, how can I trust that God loves me? Well, the most obvious and most important is His word, which is His main pathway to speak to us. I'm not implying that the Lord cannot speak by any other means, but the quickest and most efficient way is to go straight to His word. So, as we see in Ephesians 2, God is rich in mercy toward us, and His love is magnificently great. The problem, once again, is that we might read it on paper, but it has not taken hold of our mind and heart; they have not linked together as a router syncs up with several devices throughout a house. Of course, there can be disconnects, or sometimes the router might need to be upgraded, but God can link our minds and hearts together better than ever before or even upgrade (a reference for being born again) in ways we never thought possible.

When we let God's truth switch turn on the connection between our mind and heart (which can take some time) we find the divine trust in God that we were always meant to have. No longer do we have to live alienated from Him; no longer do we have to live in fear, shame, or guilt. We can approach His throne with boldness and confidence, for His word tells us to. Even if you have felt that you were on the outskirts of your faith, it is never too late to run to the throne of God with a shameless audacity, regardless of what others may think or believe. When Jesus told the woman caught in adultery (John 8:1-11) to go and sin no more, I often wonder what her immediate life was like. I can imagine people thinking or even saying aloud, "You have the audacity to show your face here? The town whore!?" The former adulterous woman, who once slept around to feel and find self-worth now could claim that this Messiah had changed her life. She had the audacity to show her face again in public? Most would have probably run away and hidden somewhere, and maybe she did.

I like to think that maybe she went back into her town a changed person, faced up to her old life, and by God's grace pursued a new one. This is what a divine trust enables us to do; it changes us from the inside out and gives us the strength to stand in the face of any circumstance that life brings us. This is exactly what Paul meant in Philippians 4:13, not that we could be the next great linebacker if we don't have the proper build for it. The Apostle Paul was a man who endured great suffering in his life (2 Corinthians 11:22-32), yet even in spite of such hardship, he continued to boast, not in himself, but in Jesus Christ. He kept going to various church bodies and reminding them about their true selves in Christ. Jesus was not some abstract or impersonal figure to him, even though he did not see Christ in the physical sense.

Some might find it alarming that he never actually saw Jesus, but we can't let that deter us from remembering our conversion process, for each of us has come face to face with the grace and presence of Jesus. It

# A Divine Trust

doesn't matter how dramatic it may be; we all don't have to be knocked on our butts as Paul was.

In his book The Case for Christ, Lee Strobel says that his conversion experience was not an emotional one, but he felt more of an assurance of who Jesus was in that he could trust Him. He, too, never saw Jesus, and I am sure that he was discipled by other believers in who Jesus was, as it relates to His love and grace, as well as solid biblical doctrine. In the same way, Paul spent time with people who knew Jesus the most, Peter, James, and John. These were all men who were hit with the divine trust that Jesus left us through the Holy Spirit (John 14:26). Were they perfect? Far from it, but I have to believe that for as much as Peter screwed up in his life, he was hit with that trust. It might have taken him to the point of denying Christ to have a moment of clarity in himself to think, "Wow, He can be trusted, and He is who He says He is!"

James, the half-brother of Jesus, originally thought Jesus was full of it (John 7:5). It's not hard to believe that His brothers and family in general thought He was nuts. But what must have clicked inside of James's soul for him to realize that his Brother wasn't, indeed, a basket case who would be probably be institutionalized by today's standards? On one hand, I believe we can only attribute that to the work of the Holy Spirit, for that is what changes the tone of one's inner disposition to start with. And, even though it is not detailed within the pages of Scripture, it is not hard for me to believe that Jesus (being human) prayed for His half-brother and the rest of His family. On the other hand, James must have been taken with utter surprise when he realized that his Brother was the One about whom the Torah prophesied and that it had all come true.

It would have been an interesting relationship, to say the least, being the brother of Jesus and also trusting and believing in Him as the Way, the Truth, and the Life. I imagine that, if James got to spend more time with his Brother, believing that He was who He claimed to be, it could have been very special as well. I personally cannot begin to understand how that relational dichotomy would even begin to work, and I'm not going to try. But I also cannot *not* believe that something clicked in the soul of James, which made him have a ruthless trust in his (half) Brother. After all, James was one of the earliest witnesses of Jesus' resurrection, (1 Corinthians 15:7), so, in many ways, one could easily categorize James as a skeptic, and if the Hound of Heaven himself can invade the heart of someone like James or even Paul, He can invade yours, too, and change your life in ways you never thought possible. Of course, the caveat must be added that some people will refuse to believe, and as such, the mad love of the Father will grievingly say, "Thy will be done." A few days ago, I watched a debate between a skeptic and a follower of Jesus. The Christ-follower asked the skeptic if he witnessed someone rise from the dead right in front of him, would he believe? The skeptic answered with a resounding no.

Of course, it becomes a very intriguing idea to believe that everyone will come to have a ruthless trust in the Savior Jesus Christ, but I do not believe that the pages of Scripture support the idea very well. I believe that God knows who will ultimately bend the knee in loving surrender and who will ultimately still clench their first regardless of what they see or hear. Because the Father knows who is His, that should not be a deterrent or an excuse not to share our light with others.

## Question for Reflection

**Be honest: What has been your level of trust in the father? For many of us, it seems to come in flux. What are some ways and areas in your life where you could trust more?**

# 17
# Light

> "So now there is no condemnation for those who belong to Christ Jesus."
>
> Romans 8:1

WHEN WE BECOME a new creation in Christ, the light of Christ radiates from within us. It seems that only recently am I truly starting to give attention to the light that God has graciously bestowed upon me because far too often my energy is spent troubled by the shame of my own sin, as well as listening to the condemnation that the enemy spews from his deceitful lips. Matthew 5 tells us that everyone should be able to see the light of Christ in us and that it is not meant to be hidden or covered up. I confess that many times, I willfully shy away from exemplifying the light of Christ because I am afraid of being seen as a fool or, worse yet, an overly religious nut. As such, I tend to speak and act as though I am not a fool for Christ and not a direct representative of His love and what He has done for me, much like Peter did.

Occurrences like this are not a one-time thing; oftentimes, I might get an inner inclination to tell someone that God loves them or remind them of the mad love of God, but I don't and choose my own cowardice instead. With every shameful occasion, though, I turn and run back to the throne of God instantly. Skeptics have often raged against this reality, claiming that it is not true or right for someone to commit such a wretched act and be forgiven in the moment. To a degree, the frustration is warranted, but there is a difference between a truly contrite heart and someone who only acts spiritually in fear of the consequences.

The psalmist David knew this very well; in fact, when you take the time to read through the Psalms, you see that David's life was full of ups and downs. He was a man deeply acquainted with his own human condition. Some people have the illusion that they are so amazing and great, often because they feel they are not like all the others who screw up on a daily basis. But I can assure you that no human being is that grandiose of a person. David knew that, too, and his words in Psalm 32:3 are proof of that; he says that "When I kept silent, my bones wasted away through my groaning all day long" (NIV). He goes on to mention that the hand of God was heavy upon him. David's sin, much like mine, hides the light of Christ. The mad love of the Father will not allow us to stay in such a dreadful and death-filled state. As such, the love-filled, heavy hand of God will be on His beloved until we can do nothing but be honest about the state of our souls.

When we allow the light of Christ to break through the darkness of our sin, only then can we say the words that David inked in Psalm 51:1-12 (ESV):

"Have mercy on me, O God,
according to your steadfast love;
according to your abundant mercy
blot out my transgressions.
Wash me thoroughly from my iniquity,
and cleanse me from my sin!
For I know my transgressions,
and my sin is ever before me.
Against you, you only, have I sinned
and done what is evil in your sight,
so that you may be justified in your words
and blameless in your judgment.
Behold, I was brought forth in iniquity,

and in sin did my mother conceive me.
Behold, you delight in truth in the inward being,
and you teach me wisdom in the secret heart.
Purge me with hyssop, and I shall be clean;
wash me, and I shall be whiter than snow.
Let me hear joy and gladness;
let the bones that you have broken rejoice.
Hide your face from my sins,
and blot out all my iniquities.
Create in me a clean heart, O God,
and renew a right spirit within me.
Cast me not away from your presence,
and take not your Holy Spirit from me.
Restore to me the joy of your salvation,
and uphold me with a willing spirit."

As broken and as foolish as David was, he is a pillar for how the light of Christ can transform a person's life, as were the apostles, Peter, Paul, James, John, and even all the women who followed Jesus (Luke 8). It bears repeating again that when you're a new creation in Christ, the old has gone and new has come (2 Corinthians 5:17). It doesn't matter your past, doesn't matter if you murdered people, were heavy into drugs, sold drugs, were a prostitute, or were addicted to porn. The mad love of God can transform even the most broken and nasty of persons. And, though it does not matter the past that we have lived, it does mean that we are filled with new desires and no longer want to appease the temptation of the old self. We must also learn that in order for our light to shine brightest, we have to put on the spiritual body armor that God has gifted us with in Ephesians 6. I am utterly convinced that at the end of our lives, nothing will matter more than what we chose to do with the love and light that God has given us. Not the money in our bank accounts, not the house we lived in, the amount of social status, or even our IQ. What will matter is how we loved those around us. Did we love as Christ loved? Or did we hold tightly onto our own bitterness, regret, hatred, and shame?

If I'm honest, I believe that is what creates eternal separation. Hell, as it were, is choosing to hold onto everything mentioned above. Holding onto all of that pain that wounds us physically, spiritually, emotionally, draining us of all vitality and flourishing. The scary reality is, though, that there are hearts that are so stubborn that no matter what is said to them or what they see with their own eyes, nothing can move or penetrate their hearts. Pharaoh in the book of Exodus is a prime example. For no matter how many chances the Father gave him to set God's people free, his response to God was "no" each time. Reading this story creates a deep spiritual sensitivity inside me for people who resound with no to the good news of Christ. In the deepest parts of me, it makes me want to give up the fight for their souls, but that also would be a grave mistake. I can remember my junior year of college, listening to a pastor talk about the power of prayer. One thing that he mentioned that truly stuck with me was that when we don't see the results, that doesn't mean that we cease praying for the hope of salvation for those we love.

Jesus commands us in the Gospels to go make disciples (Matthew 28:19-20). Well, in order to do that, we must first swallow our pride, ego, and fear, get out of our comfort zone and actually tell someone about Christ for anything to happen. Then it is, of course, up to the Spirit to move as He pleases.

## Question for Reflection

As God's light to the world, have you made the most of it? What thoughts or emotions does this reality bring out of you?

# 18
## The Spiritual Glue

> "For we are God's masterpiece. He has created us anew in Christ Jesus, so we can do the good things he planned for us long ago."
>
> Ephesians 2:10

YOU MIGHT BE READING the pages in this manuscript and have considered yourself to be a Christian your whole life, and the mad love of God seems like a brand-new idea for you. Or, you have felt that you have gone so far off the beaten path that you don't know which way is home. Scripture tells us to approach the throne of God with confidence (Hebrews 4:16). On one hand, this passage provides the soul with a great deal of comfort. On the other hand, an antagonist speaks up from within me who says, "You have the audacity to approach God after sinning moments ago?"

My response to the antagonizing voice, "Yes, He (God) tells me to …"

The antagonist then replies, "No way, you should at least clean yourself up before you even think about approaching God."

Me: "Not exactly…for I cannot make myself spotless as He can. I can only do my best by His grace to repent and resist my sin." I tend to listen to that ongoing dialogue in my soul on a fairly regular basis. Sometimes I try to ignore it and proceed on in my pursuit of God. Other times it becomes so overbearing that I imagine trying to cover up cover my ears to block out the enemy and all his lies. My only assurance in these times is that God will hold me together, as a person uses a strong glue to hold something together. For He holds everything together. Some days I wake up thinking that I have made too many wrong choices in life, and thus the chance of my life amounting to something is a shot in the dark. But what kind of God would God be if He wasn't bigger or more powerful than my choices? The reality of the love of God and the Gospel is that it doesn't depend on us. It doesn't depend on our effort, our spiritual resume, our spiritual fervor, or piety.

As Tim Keller puts it, "The great basis of Christian assurance is not how much our hearts are set on God, but how unshakably His heart is set on us." It would be easy to think, then, that a Christ-follower can live a lazy and careless life, without the formation of spiritual discipline and desire in one's life, but that would be a mistake in understanding the mad love of the Father. Yet, there is nothing we can do to earn or lose His love, and because He loved us to the point of taking the world's sin and brokenness upon Himself, He conquered death and the eternal consequences of our sin in order that we may be new creations and the beloved in Christ Jesus.

Though this reality is true, I still find myself doubting and being filled with unbelief. I find myself praying and doubting that God hears me or will do anything. In many ways, it is possible to be a professing believer in Jesus and function as an agnostic. When I first realized this very disposition in my heart, I felt a lot like Peter after he realized that he had denied Christ even when he said he never would. In the same way, I have lost faith after being a spiritually filled Christian, on a high, thinking I would never be in such a place. In these moments, I cry out to the Father, asking and pleading that He holds me together. Even more so, for those around me whom I love, that He would be at work in their lives, revealing His mad love to them.

I often struggle and wrestle with thoughts of the afterlife, as it relates to those around me. I cringe at the idea of eternal separation, which I believe to be a reality. I'm not sure how one could look at

Scripture and see otherwise, but there are, in fact, pastors who believe that eternal separation is not real and that in the end, God's love will melt all the hearts of all people. Again, do I believe this to be true? NO, I do NOT. But does the thought, idea, or reality seem very appealing to me? YES, there has been much thought given on the topic; it is immensely comforting to me, but once again I do not believe it to be true. In my estimation, there is no proof in Scripture that God even gives people second chances. It sounds amazingly great, and it would most certainly take away any and all spiritual and emotional anxiety, but it is still a huge gamble, especially as it relates to being lights for the Gospel and obeying the Great Commission.

We are to go unto all the world with our light, and I think it's extremely vital to note that in that same vein of thought, that then makes us all (followers of Christ) missionaries. As cliché as this statement is, being a missionary does not mean that you have to sell all your belongings and go to a third-world country, though that may, in fact, be your calling. The people in our homes and our communities are the mission field, so to speak. I have sometimes felt, that in some ways, in speaking of the mission field, people become tasks, rather than people with stories, hopes, dreams, and so on. I was once of the mindset of, "I have to convert you," but in reality, it's more like, "I want you to see and fall in love so deeply with the mad love of God that nothing else even compares."

In my first Bible college, we had to go out and tell five people about God; there was no clear-cut formula. We just had to do it. I remember being barely twenty-something and using the antagonist approach, as one who was tired of having religious belief imposed upon him. In a few of my conversations, some people said, "Yeah, man, that really sucks hope you figure that **** out." Other times, I would simply ask people how they felt about God. One young woman smiled at me and said, "I think God is awesome and that He loves everyone." Her answer made me smile, but part of me wishes that I could go back to that moment and tell her about the mad love of the Father. For it is one thing to say that God loves everyone and another to know of His love in a deep and personal way. I have a handful of people in my life whom I would love to tell of the Father's love, but my fear is that they will not listen, nor do I have a compelling philosophical or scientific argument to combat them with. I only have the mad love of God, whose love roars like a lion. As the Apostle Paul graciously said, "And my message and my preaching were very plain. Rather than using clever and persuasive speeches, I relied only on the power of the Holy Spirit." (1 Corinthians 2:4, NLT).

More often than not, when I do not have the words, my weapon of choice is prayer. Furthermore, I cling to the reality that God is the glue that holds everything together, the One who controls. And I pray for those in my life who do not believe in the mad love of the Father, that they would be melted by the love of God while they are still alive, and that the flame that was once quenched would burn brighter than ever.

## Question for Reflection

Do you honestly know and believe that you are secure in the father? Do you know that you are his?

# 19
# Awaiting the New You

> "Every parting gives a foretaste of death, every reunion a hint of the resurrection."
>
> Arthur Schopenhauer

WITHIN THE HUMAN CONDITION, there arises a moment in time in which we want to be our healthiest physically, mentally, and even spiritually. I would argue that spiritual needs have just as much precedence as the previous two components to our health. If you think about a couple who are madly in love and have set a date when they will become one in marriage, they each want to look their best for their grand day, and, as such, both set out to start taking care of themselves in ways they never did before. They start going to the gym to shed pounds and fat on their bodies, they start eating cleaner, and they even put aside previous addictive patterns to be the best that they can be. Most people tend to do this, and then, after a few years, children show up in the picture and that healthy lifestyle seems to take the back seat in the name of putting your beloved children before your own needs.

The moment we decide to start implementing the discipline to take care of our spiritual selves on a daily basis, especially in terms of a wedding, has much more significance than any earthly one. Scripturally speaking, our Lord is the groom, and His beloved is the body of Christ, the Church, you, and me. And because of His mad love, we must see again that He has made us new creations, spiritually speaking, in Christ Jesus. In that same train of thought comes what reformers call new desires, where we no longer crave or desire the same things we did before. We now desire the things that please God, seeking Him daily for our joy, happiness, and purpose. That is not to imply that other earthly people, places, or things that bring us joy, happiness, and purpose are bad, but anything that we utterly depend on for those things, beyond the mad love of God, is foolishness and sin. For we know that other people and things, in some way shape, or form, let us down in the end, break, or cease to function. Yet we become so enthralled with new experiences that we succumb to the belief that they will satisfy us, and they will, but only for a moment. Through the desires of Christ, however, we understand that only He can bring us lasting satisfaction; even when we are like the prodigal son and decide that it might be a good idea to run away from home, we come to our true sense of where we really belong. Yet the new you, the new me, should be craving the same things that God wants, which is to be more like His Son Jesus. Why? Because when we are with Christ in all His glory, we will be free of sin, suffering, and all other forms of brokenness that encompass the world we live in. (1 Corinthians 15:52).

Many people who have faced various forms of suffering all of our lives, cerebral palsy, arthritis, mental illness, chronic pain, or whatever you choose to add to the immensely wide and complex list, long to be free from suffering and experience existence without such pain. I, for one, long to be rid of cerebral palsy, to be able to run, jump, do back flips, and so on. I know someone who has a very painful form of arthritis; it sucks the energy right of her and has even left her screaming due to the pain. Or think of the young child who has several hundred seizures a day and can't have any sense of normalcy in life. These examples only scratch the surface, as it pertains to those of us who live with serious medical issues every day of our lives. Not every day is bad; in fact, some days I'll bet some of us can find a sense of joy, and if you're a parent of one with special needs, I'm sure that you're thankful for the days that go a bit more smoothly.

Others of us, though, long for freedom from our darkest addictions. If you have wrestled against the temptation of alcoholism, pornography, various drug addictions, self-harm, and so on, you know what I mean. In these contexts, perhaps something led you to go down these destructive paths. Whatever it may be, maybe it was deep loneliness that drove you to choose one of these destructive ways of coping. Or maybe you simply desired some form of acceptance, community, and love that you never had before. Going a step further, maybe you have felt like you were never good enough anyway, and so your drug of choice became food, largely because it was easily available to you. Food addiction obviously manifests itself in different ways, meaning the end result is different. While some eat for the sake of comfort, some don't eat at all for the fear of how food might make them appear to others. Every destructive cycle of behavior can wreak havoc on the body, mind, and emotions, to the point of feeling like your being is crumbling from underneath you.

In my own struggle with lust, the shame has sometimes been so much that all I want to do is curl up in bed all day and not come out. I'm sure that the person who has eaten themselves into a place of immense obesity feels the same way in some regard. They wish they weren't that way, probably don't want to be seen by the world, and even have considered taking their own life. Maybe you can relate to this as well; I know I can. When your mind and body are so deeply affected by addiction or the consequences of careless living, something inside you longs for a new, healthy body. Depending on one's own interpretation, I take the Scripture to mean that we will indeed have new bodies once we are in the full presence of God, within eternity's context. I remember once reading a story about a Baptist lady who also seemed to have a very charismatic background; she spoke in her article about how she could not wait to be free from her earthly body and enter her new one. She also had a host of health issues, the biggest I believe being type one diabetes. One thing she said that struck me was that due to the fact that she was getting a new, heavenly body in eternity, she didn't need to worry about what happened in her earthly body. On one hand, she is correct because if we have Christ, it does not matter if we face cancer, various diseases, mental illness, and even death. If we are truly in Christ, nothing can ever remove us from His love (Romans 8:31-39). This becomes our greatest source of joy, hope, and strength because we know that we will have victory through Him in the end.

On the other hand, I believe that there is a sense of faulty logic in her thinking. The faulty logic comes in thinking that we should not have a holy amount of concern for what happens in our bodies. What I mean by holy concern is that on one hand our bodies are gifts, and we should do our best to take care of and honor them. On the other hand, our bodies are a temporary temple or home, and we ought to keep the inside and outside clean at the same time. Jesus at one point even rebuked the religious leaders of His day for appearing to be holy on the outside but on the inside being full of darkness (Matthew 23:25). I once heard it said that the body is not a temple, but a fun house. Meaning that we should seek as much pleasure and experience as we can possibly handle.

If we are truly honest with ourselves, this is a very sad reality to live in. Many of us think that having a sense of restriction or discipline means a lack of freedom, joy, and pleasure. But that's just not true. The idea that we must seek out our every heart's desire, as we have throughout the last several years of history, only leads to a grave end. Often, I find that those who seek the most earthly treasure and pleasure are those who are not tending to the deep vacuum inside the soul. The vacuum I speak of is one that sucks all mental, emotional, and spiritual vitality away. Even when we have the pleasure and possession, it may last for a while, but in the end, it leaves us like a car stranded on the side of the road with no fuel to go further. I truly believe that the deepest satisfaction is when we know the truth. We are changed from the inside out. And it is within that perspective that we start to see that restricting ourselves from some things and saying no to other things, in the name of discipline, is also an act of love and freedom. Can we still have moments in life where we are filled with what seems to be an unquenchable thirst? Yes. Can we still have moments when we feel lonely and panic-ridden? Yes. Will we still have moments where jumping back into the skin of the old you seem plausible? Yes, but now we have a well to draw from in the mad love of God.

## Question for Reflection

Do you find yourself eager to be with Christ in eternity? And knowing that a resurrected body is part of it.

# 20
# The Heavy Soul

> "Why, my soul, are you downcast? Why so disturbed within me? Put your hope in God, for I will yet praise him, my Savior and my God."
> Psalm 42:11

AS A CHRISTIAN who has lived with depression and anxiety for most of my life, I have been to a handful of counselors and tried a few different medications. I also am not one who thinks that a person who calls themselves a Christian and takes medication along with counseling is lacking in faith. Those things might actually help shine a light on the heaviness of the soul. Yet, I will boldly submit to you that nothing has helped me, in my journey with mental illness, more than the Psalms. The poetry-filled pages speak of sadness, despair, longing, joy, hopefulness, rejection, doubt, vengeance, and more. Each time I start to make my way through each section, I can feel the mad love of God propelling me to come before Him, regardless of what I may be feeling at a given moment.

He shines a lantern of hope into my heavy soul, causing me to follow the Good Shepherd upon still waters (Psalm 23). That being said, however, I know what it is like to feel as though there is no God. And if there is, then He must be a million miles from you. I know what it is like to feel as though there is no meaning or grand design to life. I know how it feels to be despairing of your own life and feel as if the world is better off without you or that no one sees you. The heavy soul is no hindrance to the mad love of God. He doesn't tell us to be less anxious or filled with sorrow before we come before Him. No, He calms our anxious hearts and wipes away every sorrow. There are times throughout my life where my own depression has been so heavy, but I only knew how to pack it down, as a soldier packs down black powder in an old-fashioned rifle. High-functioning depression is a condition I have often experienced. For me, this means being able to get out of bed (when I'd rather sleep the whole day). I work out and shower. I do my best to appear normal, but that doesn't always pay off with certain people in life. Other times, I am able to put a smile on my face and appear optimistic and godly. Inwardly, though, my soul and mind feel as though they are like a bridge ready to collapse.

The Psalms have taught me that I don't have to pretend that life is always so colorful, that life does in fact have really dark caves of pain, suffering, and hopelessness, but that I can rest on the heart of God, even in the midst of such darkness. To this day, I still feel that there are many people who feel like outcasts from the church, regardless of whether they go to church every Sunday, or they haven't been to church in over twenty years. It can be easy to feel like an outcast, if you feel more down than up, if you have more apparent doubt than you do trust, or if you have even more of a longing to depart from life than you do joy in life. The body of Christ could do a far greater job of knowing how to be present in the company of one with a heavy soul.

I have often felt a plague of guilt because I don't often feel happy due to something or some type of turmoil going on within me. I think, however, that simply because a Christian is not outwardly radiant does not mean that there is not a deep understanding and trust of the mad love of God. Jesus, after all, was called a man of sorrows (Isaiah 53). When, by God's grace, I was made alive by His Spirit, suddenly I became keenly aware of just how deeply the world was broken due to sin. Before I was a Christian, there was a sense in me that the world sucked and was a very dark and nasty place. Yet, when I became a Christian, that reality went way deeper. I realized that every part of the human condition and nature is broken, which sounds like a very pointless, hopeless, and grim reality. The Christian reality makes us all look with focused eyes on this understanding. Solomon himself said that everything under the sun is meaningless unless you are pursuing God (my paraphrase). For the heavy and depressed soul, it can seem sometimes like God is a million miles away or there is no God at all. But when we dive headfirst into the poetry of the Psalms, we can see that David felt the exact same things we humans feel and face today.

The Psalms are not merely spiritual platitudes that well-intended Christians share, but they are a diving board into the warmth of God's mad love for us. When the soul is downcast, we need to swim longer in the Lord's presence and affection for us. Of course, the human soul is far more than just chemicals and emotions, and the heavy soul is more than a spiritual component, but a physical, emotional, and spiritual trifecta at the same time. When I was finishing up my college degree, there was a time when I was so spiritually and emotionally despondent that nothing made sense to me. I felt that I was a lab rat trapped in a maze. But what I realized was that I needed more than a sermon. I needed proper rest and nutrition.

This reality came to me when I was reading 1 Kings 19, the section where the prophet Elijah is on the run for his life. Jezebel had already slain other prophets by the sword, and now Elijah was on the run. In Verse 4 it reads, "But he himself went a day's journey into the wilderness, and sat under a broom tree. And he prayed that he might die and said, 'It is enough! Lord, take my life, for I am no better than my fathers'" (ESV). In the following verses, Elijah goes in and out of sleep. Then an angel appears to him and is sure to make him eat, drink, and sleep. It is important to note that in the particular context, the angel that was sent to him did not give him a lecture on how he needed to have more faith or be more fearless in the Lord. But the angel seems to have had a more gentle and compassionate demeanor toward the heavy soul of Elijah. As Tim Keller puts it, "Sometimes you need a sermon, and other times you need a nice meal and walk by the sea." When one has a heavy soul like Elijah, especially if one is Abba's child, you need to be reminded of His mad love for you.

You must look three times more closely at who Jesus is and what He has done for you.

## Question for Reflection

Depression and anxiety are still somewhat taboo subjects in the Church, so many of us stay silent about it. How have depression and anxiety affected your life? Do you feel comfortable discussing it with fellow Christians? Has mental health impacted your walk with God?

# 21
# For the Sensitive Soul

"Since we live by the Spirit, let us keep in step with the Spirit."
Galatians 5:25

I HAVE a very sensitive soul. I feel things very deeply and sometimes find myself wanting to be away from the world. Oftentimes I am filled with regret over things from my past. Another way of putting it is that I have a heart filled full of condemnation, even though I know the pure sweetness of Romans 8:1-2, which says there is therefore now NO CONDEMNATION to those who are in Christ Jesus, who do not walk according to the flesh, but according to the Spirit. For the law of the Spirit of life in Christ Jesus has made me free from the law of sin and death. Even with such a glorious proclamation, it is easy for me to think that that is applicable for others but not me. It is easy to think that God hates you and that you still deserve the guilt, shame, and condemnation on a daily basis. Maybe if you're like me you still find yourself mentally beating yourself in the head for saying or doing something you shouldn't have. Or someone said something to you that hurt, and over time you realized just how deeply it actually hurt. Going further, if you believe that we have a real spiritual enemy (Satan), then you know very well that he likes to remind us of how we have fallen short and that we don't measure up. Scripture tells us that the enemy comes to kill, steal, and destroy (John 10:10).

The other side of that verse says, in the words of Jesus, I have come that you may have life and life to the full. If I am painfully honest, it is far easier to listen to the lies of the enemy than the truth of what God says about me. It's easier to listen to the lies, lies that say that no one loves you, that you're too much of a screw-up, or that God really doesn't love you. Most days the sensitivity in my own soul is so great that it almost keeps me from functioning to my fullest. Some days I would not even want to face the day because the condemnation is so much. In my own shame and sensitivity, the enemy whispers cleverly in my ear: You're not a Christian; you're a fake and a horrible example. To pour a sense of calm or a warm balm on the heart of a sensitive soul, the mad love of God has nothing to do with shame or condemnation, for Scripture says that it is His kindness that leads us to repentance (Romans 2:4).

The mad love of God convicts our souls when we have done something wrong, but it does not torture us by constantly reminding us of our failures. Scripture tells us that God disciplines those He loves (Romans 2:4); discipline, though it can be firm, is not the same as the enemy's tactics. He takes things that have hints of truth and amplifies them. Often, when I say or do something that is against who I truly am, after a bit of time passes, I can feel the warm hand of God upon me, correcting me and moving me to repentance. Or, when some situation in my past keeps coming up in my mind, I am utterly convinced that it is the mad love of God guiding me to make peace with whatever keeps coming to mind. This sensitivity of the soul is not something to be ashamed of or withdraw from, but something to be embraced, cherished and even rejoiced in. The sensitivity to the things of God is, in my opinion, a sign that you are spiritually healthy, for spiritually healthy people understand when they have sinned against God and others.

In these times, I cry out, "O, Abba please forgive me! I have been a fool once again." And, as close as breath, the mad love of God is there to cleanse and forgive me. It is a mad love and a shameless audacity, as it were, to know that God is so filled with love and desire for humanity to know how to find lasting joy and peace that He would send His Son into this broken world as the God-MAN Jesus Christ, to live among us broken people, to show us that He is the way to God and not merely some enlightened spiritual guru. My sensitive soul weeps happily to know that Jesus was not afraid to hang out with people who have been sexually promiscuous, diseased, physically handicapped in some ways, the addicted, the mentally unstable, outcasts, and more. To most people who do not know the mad love of God, that in itself is audacity, the idea that a sinner can do something so hideous and be forgiven and cleansed at a moment's notice.

      To an extent, they're right. It is utter madness to think that God in His love can forgive in the blink of an eye. Yet, to the sensitive soul, it is the most precious gift because I am a mad lover of God who sins every day! Scripture tells us that we are to approach the throne of God with confidence (Hebrews 4:16). When our hearts condemn us, the sensitive soul must find its weapons. My first very weapon is 1 John 3:20: "If our hearts condemn us, we know that God is greater than our hearts, and He knows everything" (NIV). God is greater than our hearts! Greater than our crippling thoughts and emotions that we can cling to and rejoice in. My second weapon of choice is none other than Ephesians 6. The whole chapter is amazing, and I would encourage the sensitive soul to dwell in that passage daily. My third weapon of choice is 1 Corinthians 4:3-4: "But with me it is a very small thing that I should be judged by you or by a human court. In fact, I do not even judge myself. For I know of nothing against myself, yet I am not justified by this; but He who judges me is the Lord" (ESV).

In the words of Tim Keller, Paul is saying that he doesn't care what people say about him; he doesn't even care about what he thinks about himself, but he does care about what He (God) thinks. As sensitive souls, it can be far too easy to let the harsh criticisms of others stick to us. They can often haunt us, and then when we judge ourselves as well, we only add to the pain, regret, shame, grief, or whatever it may be. Martin Luther, before he knew deeply of God's grace, would literally whip himself in order to show God just how sorry he was for his sins, but when he began to truly look at the mad love that God had for him, he put down that whip. And we must do the same. I have spent far too much of life holding onto negative things that people have said about me, and even more time beating myself up, mentally speaking, and much less time looking at what God thinks of me and the mad love that He has for me in spite of how big of a screw up I am. His mad love tells me to come to Him with a shameless audacity. The poetry of Psalms 103:11-12 reads, "For as the heavens are high above the earth, so great is His mercy toward them that fear Him. As far as the east is from the west, so far hath he removed our transgressions from us" (KJV). For the sensitive soul, I feel there needs to be a small note regarding the word fear. There is no contradiction of terms here; the mad love of God tells us to go to Him with confidence and a shameless audacity, but the fear that Scripture speaks of is one of awe and reverence because God is holy and powerful. In this light, the sensitive soul can see the Father as a mighty warrior and protector, not simply as an angry father who is constantly grumpy or irritated.

    I think that so many people get hung up on the fear of God in the Bible versus the fear that they have of their earthly father. For the sake of healthy spirituality, as a child of God, there must be a distinction. Yes, the mad love of God does have indignation toward those stubborn hearts, who at the end of time still refuse to acknowledge what they already know in their hearts, but when you're in Christ, there is no condemnation for you! (Romans 8). Our heavenly Daddy does not get annoyed, irritated, or cranky when we ask things of Him. I knew someone once whose father was a pretty heavy alcoholic, who had a deep anger issue. When this person would give a testimony to a room of high school students, there would not be a dry eye because he would tell a story about how he and his brother would ask their father for food, and the father would become so annoyed that he would grab both his sons by their ankles and hang them over the deck and say, "ARE YOU STILL HUNGRY!?" Sadly, there are other fathers like this in our world, but the beauty of this person's story was that as he grew, he learned with God's grace to forgive. His father has met the mad love of God and is a changed person. Perhaps you have a father like the one described above. Maybe there is a relationship fracture, and you may feel that it can never be repaired. I, too, am painfully aware of how hopeless a situation like that can feel, but more often than not, we have to switch how we feel for what God says is true, and the mad love of God says that nothing is impossible with Him (Luke 1:37). The mad love of God can heal any relationship by the power of His Spirit.

Many times it requires us to put aside our pride, ego, and stubbornness in humility and submit ourselves before God. A friend of mine and I, while were still in college, simply could not see eye-to-eye on almost anything. For a great amount of time, we did not speak or have any form of communication, but somehow the Spirit of God brought us back together. From time to time, we still have our moments of frustration and disagreement, but we have both learned to take a deep breath and forgive each other. I am proud to say that he is one of my best friends. With the sensitive soul, it is so easy to feel the pain of brokenness in our lives and the lives of others, which is why it is so intrinsically important to spend time being caught up in the mad love of the Father.

It's okay to find a quiet place for your soul to rest in God. Jesus tells us to cast all our cares upon Him because He cares for us (1 Peter 5:7). So, if you have a fractured relationship with your father or even your mother, they are never too far out of God's reach. We must never cast someone out of God's reach, even though our minds may tell us that it is utterly impossible. We must never allow the enemy the chance to distract us or harden our hearts for too long. Even in my own bitter, hard-hearted ways, I can feel the kindness of God, telling me and teaching me to be sensitive to His Spirit and the pain of others. As it relates to being a sensitive soul, we must be sensitive to God and others. I must say that it is okay to cry and let out the pain within. The shortest verse in the Bible says that Jesus wept (John 11:35). Jesus even wept over Jerusalem because of the hardness of their hearts (Luke 13:34). Jesus very much understands the pain, agony, and grief when people are far too stiff-necked to come before the throne of God for repentance and renewal. He even weeps with you over the broken relationships between people and family members. I truly believe that He even weeps over people who hang onto their bitterness and hatred of one another.

The only cure for stubborn, bitter, and broken hearts is the mad love of God. I truly believe that all people need to know that the only true way to happiness and healing of pain is colliding with the mad love of God and letting Him turn your life upside down and inside out.

## Question for Reflection

If you are like me, you have a sensitive heart. Have you seen it as a blessing or not? Better yet, how can we all be more sensitive to the moving of the Holy Spirit in our lives?

# 22
# Silencing the Enemy

> "You, dear children, are from God and have overcome them because the one who is in you is greater than the one who is in the world."
>
> 1 John 4:4

I DO NOT WISH for anyone to be naïve, as fierce as the mad love of God actually is. There is, in fact, a grim and grave enemy. One of darkness and not of light. This enemy is a liar; he can twist the truth to poke and stab away at our souls. For in my darkest moments of despair, the enemy reminds me that I am a horrible person whom God doesn't actually love. On the one hand, there is a hint of truth there—I am in fact a horrible person outside of Christ, who is only focused on his own desires and self. I truly am a person who wants to be his own god, and if I am deeply honest, in my depravity, people become a means to an end. Yet the distinction then is, when one becomes a new creation, by the triumphant power of the Holy Spirit the Lord sees us as He sees His Son, Jesus.

For some time, one of my greatest fears was that I would be one of the people that God told, "Depart from me, for I never knew you" (Matthew 7:21-23). I would imagine standing before the Lord and Him looking at me with grieved eyes, saying nope, not you, and as I turn around in disgrace, the Lord gives me a firm boot in the backside. To this day, this fear still lingers, but it is not as bad as it once was. Rather than letting this fear paralyze me, I have learned to engage heavily in spiritual combat. The armor and weapon that I use are not of my own strength and design but are given by the greatest Commander of all,

Jesus Christ. Ephesians 6 says in Verse 10, "Finally, my brethren, be strong in the Lord and in the power of His might." The first and most crucial element that we most notice is that when we are engaged in spiritual combat, it is not actually our strength that matters in the fight, but more so an utter dependence on the mercy, love, and grace of the Lord Jesus. Even when I think that I am swinging the spiritual sword that God has given me, I firmly believe that it is Him wielding the sword for me, as a father gets behind his son or daughter to teach them how to swing a bat or racket. The heavenly Father does not leave us on our own as orphans, to learn how to defend our minds and hearts. It is my conviction that God is always fighting for us, always fighting for our good, and always fighting for us to be more like His Son Jesus, every single day. Growing up in the spiritual sense, my first church was a very Assembly of God/Pentecostal setting. The pastors and community there believed heavily in spiritual warfare and speaking in tongues.

I can remember being in youth group on a Wednesday night, and the pastor had just gotten word that our soldiers were at war in Iraq. He quickly stopped his message and told us that it was time for spiritual warfare, so we all stretched out our hands to Heaven and prayed for all the brave men and women going head and heart first into battle. I believe that in spite of growing up in this way, the enemy does everything that he can to distract me from the spiritual reality of life, that it is good versus evil, darkness and light, and even angels and demons. The lie here, in my mind at least, is that there is no spiritual realm and that prayer and spiritual warfare don't matter. Many people speak of having one life to live, living life to the fullest, squeezing every second out of life that we can. And to a degree, I agree with these philosophies and perspectives on life, but I think that the enemy's goal is to get us to focus on the here and now so that we don't think about eternity and what happens when we die.

I'm not simply trying to appeal to emotion, but rather trying to get others to seriously consider the weight of our words and actions. I was once arguing with a friend who did not share my same convictions. I was of the viewpoint of wanting a sense of justice, especially for families or people who have had incredible evil done against them. The friend I was arguing with said that there was justice and consequences, in that people who commit evil acts are then subjected to prison time and even the death penalty. He's right on one hand, but on the other hand, I think his heart, mind, and eyes are blind to things much deeper. I pushed a bit further, giving the analogy of a perpetrator getting off the hook and having no remorse for his actions on his deathbed. My friend said, "Who cares? He's dead!" "Ok," I nodded, "and what about the family who has to live with the aftermath of an evil act? What about the grief that they will have to deal with? How does your perspective offer them peace?"

His response was simple, we can give them humanism, he said in response. Humanism, in simple terms, is to focus on a human (and not divine) way of solving life's problems, as well as focusing on human potential. Secular humanism, to be exact. On the other hand, Christian humanism is centered on God (divine) and is focused on humanity's unique and God-gifted purpose. It is focused on getting people to engage with the Scriptures in their own language. Can you now see what the enemy is doing here? Two spiritual forces are at war. Consider the two following passages:

1 John 5:19, "We know that we are from God, and the whole world lies in the power of the evil one" (ESV) and Revelation 12:9, "And the great dragon was thrown down, that ancient serpent, who is called the devil and Satan, the deceiver of the whole world—he was thrown down to the earth, and his angels were thrown down with him" (ESV).

As much as I have spent time trying to get closer to the mad love of God and resemble Christ to the world, the question arises, why, God, did you allow an evil force like Satan to exist in the first place? If he is a liar and a tempter, why not just end him? As Bruce Lee says in *Enter the Dragon Now*, why doesn't someone take a 45 and BANG! Settle it? It would be a noble concept, after all. All our temptations would vanish from our lives, all struggle and hardship would be gone, and people would no doubt believe that God is good. But life isn't like that, and many of us do struggle in various ways, which leaves us to ask the question: God, are you MAD? And, in a way, I would say that God is mad, crazy even, yet we as humans do mad and crazy things to express deep love and affection for another person.

God is mad about you. Know how much He loves you and the price that His Son paid for you. He is passionate about you finding your true self in Him as you were created to do. He is passionately and madly bent on us being spotless and holy in His sight. And He has gone to great lengths to reveal that to hearts that are open to receiving it. A fair amount of people in life would agree that we learn the greatest lessons about ourselves, other people, and the world around us through hardship and struggle. I have even heard famous people say that they love struggle; they love being able to persevere and figure out a solution to whatever problems they may encounter throughout their lives.

In the same way, we learn things not only about ourselves but also about the character of who God is through struggle, temptation, doubt, loneliness, and so on. When Jesus was tempted by the enemy for forty days (Matthew 4:1-4), He held the line and not only silenced the enemy by resisting the temptation that the enemy was placing in front of Him, but He also silenced the enemy by fighting back with the truth. This should not only give us the courage to stand firm against the temptation in our own lives, but also the fact that Jesus was tempted in the same ways that we assure us that we can cling to Him for strength when we find ourselves knee-deep in the fight. When we feel alone, as though the light is quickly fading, the enemy's lies and distractions can feel most real, true, and even more powerful. We may feel that we cannot fight back, but the truth is that we can because God does not abandon us in the fight. The reality is that when we are tempted to despair, we must train ourselves to surround ourselves with the shadow of His mad love for us, as well as disciplining ourselves to armor up every single day, for every day is a fight to set aside ourselves and be transformed by the mad love of God. This does not mean, then, that there will not be days of joy and moments where the presence of God seems closest.

These are days that I have come to cherish – when the mind is clear and there is no condemnation in the heart. The one thing that I have come to notice is that if we are not watchful over ourselves, the enemy is, and it is in these moments that the enemy is planning his next attack. At this point, I think it's safe to say that we have been enlisted into a fight. But it is a fight in which we can trust in the end result, and that is that the enemy will be completely and utterly finished (Revelation 20:10). So when our hearts are dismayed, let us remember the words the poet David wrote in Psalm 121:1-4:

"I lift my eyes up to the mountains-where does my help come from? My help comes from the Lord, the Maker of Heaven and earth. He will not let my foot slip—he who watches over you will not slumber; indeed, he who watches over Israel will neither slumber nor sleep" (NIV).

I believe that a vast number of Christ-followers have not only forgotten who they are in Christ, but we have forgotten that we are spiritual warriors in Christ, who fight with weapons, not of this world, and we fight an enemy that is not of this world (Ephesians 6:12). But, once again, I submit to you that we are not powerless. For our power is in Jesus' name. A lyric from the song "Your Great Name" by Natalie Grant is so fitting in this current moment that we find ourselves in. "Every fear has no place, at the sound of Your great name. The enemy, he has to leave, at the sound of Your great name." The Lord has obviously blessed her with one amazing voice, but what is she truly saying here? She is saying that our fears don't have the final say; she is saying that every lie that the enemy speaks has no final say in our lives. For we do not even have to give the enemy a second of power in our lives. The Bible tells us to not even give the enemy a foothold (Ephesians 4:27).

In the perspective of Brazilian Jiujitsu, we talk about keeping your elbows in and knowing where your feet are at all times, thus preventing an attacker from having the ability to get a submission on us. The same application applies to us in a spiritual sense, when it comes to the enemy of our souls. We have to be on guard, watchful, and mindful. We must know ourselves and how we are most easily weakened and tempted. And, on the subject of temptation, we must resist with everything we have. Hebrews 12:4 tells us, you have not resisted bloodshed, striving against sin. I think that what this passage hints at is Jesus praying in the garden (Matthew 26: 36-46). In this passage, the Lord Jesus was close to the unfolding of what would happen next. In the following chapters of Matthew's Gospel, He would be betrayed, arrested, beaten by cold-hearted soldiers, mocked, abandoned by those close to Him, and killed in the most savage and public way. By Crucifixion.

In the garden, if we were to watch from a third-party perspective, we can almost see Him in sorrow and anguish. People often mock Him, by claiming that if He is God, why then is He so afraid? Skeptics often forget that Jesus is the God-man, both God and man in the same body. Both skeptics and Christians alike forget a gem hidden in Philippians, in 2:5-7, where Paul speaks these following words to us, " Let this mind be in you which was also in Christ Jesus, who, being in the form of God, did not consider it robbery to be equal with God, but made himself of no reputation, taking the form of a bondservant and coming in the likeness of men" (NKJV). Other translations say that He emptied Himself. Some believe that Jesus emptied Himself of some of His divine attributes, but that does not correspond well with the rest of Scripture. Jesus still was able to heal others; He still knew things before others around Him even knew what would take place. The book of Hebrews tells us that Jesus never changes (Hebrews 13:8). It would not be consistent to think that Jesus gave up parts of who He is or that He forfeited parts of who He is.

Rather, it does make sense, then, that He only added the parts of being human onto Himself, which then would cause it to make sense that He felt crippling fear in the garden, to begin with. For, once again, Scripture tells us that He was tempted in every way ( Hebrews 4:15), so it is not as though the mad love of God is a remote thing that we have to do all the right things to get the attention of. Rather, Scripture tells us that knowledge of God is known to us (Romans 1:18-23), perhaps more on that in the coming pages, but the fact is that Jesus knows us, the mad love of God knows us. It isn't as though God's inner disposition is one of apathy, but He knows, for He is near to the brokenhearted (Psalm 34:18). He weeps, as we have seen in previous chapters; He weeps over the stubbornness of human hearts and the brokenness of the human condition. It is important to recall, once again, that Christ has overcome all of this misery.

The greatest symbolism apart from His love shown on the cross is depicted in The Passion of the Christ, directed by Mel Gibson. We see that after Jesus is done shaking with paralyzing fear, He is strengthened (this after the enemy has finished speaking lies in His ear). Satan lets a snake slither its way to the Messiah, Jesus. He then demonstrates that He can silence the enemy's lies and attacks, by emphatically and forcefully crushing the snake's head. Because He has done this for us, it is His strength and grace that enables and empowers us to do the same, which makes us more than conquerors in Christ Jesus.

## Question for Reflection

What lies does the enemy put in your mind? Write them down; maybe even share with someone you trust. More importantly, learn to combat the lies of the truth, community, and the armor of God.

# 23
# The God Who Haunts

> "I am he whom thou sleekest! Thou dravest love from thee, who dravest me."
> Francis Thompson, *Hound of Heaven*

I CAN REMEMBER growing up unsure that God existed, though there was something inside me that was vaguely spiritual, meaning that I thought or knew that there was something more than just the world I lived in, and more than making money, trying to thrive and eventually passing on. But passing on to what, though? Surely, if I didn't believe in God, then it didn't make sense to spend eternity with a deity that I thought sick, twisted, and cruel. As a kid, my mom would say a standard prayer before I went to sleep; you know, the standard prayer of:

Now I lay me down to sleep

If I die before I wake, I pray the Lord, my soul to take.

These words can be comforting to the soul, but as I grew older and began to experience the pain and even lonely recovery from having major surgeries on my spine, legs and hips (see my first book *The Emotional Struggle* for more details), I began to think that a God who would allow a human to go through such agony was deeply uncalled for, let alone a place where there was supposedly no more pain and everyone sat on clouds and played harps. Obviously, now, I understand that that line of thinking is incredibly wrong, for the presence of God is infinitely better than anything that our minds can draw up on our own, yet, there are those who think that Heaven is just how I described it above—boring.

## The God Who Haunts

They think that God is cruel and nasty, but I think that deep down, they want to experience and know the mad love of God. For I truly believe that everyone wants and longs to be loved from the depths of the earth to the highest Heavens. The truest reality, though, is that our hearts and minds are darkened because of our brokenness. In the previous chapter, I briefly mentioned Romans 1 and how the visible attributes (mainly creation) are known to us, Verses 20-21 read as follows:

"For since the creation of the world His invisible attributes are clearly seen, being understood by the things that are made, even His eternal power and Godhead, so that they are without excuse because, although they knew God, they did not glorify Him as God, nor were thankful, but became futile in their thoughts, and their foolish hearts were darkened" (NKJV).

It's as though the mad love of God is whispering, you know I'm real, so open up and let me in. But we don't, for in our pride we do above and beyond what it takes to resist that something in our hearts that tells us so. This is why Verse 21 says that although they knew God, they did not glorify Him as God, nor were they thankful, but became futile in their thoughts and their foolish hearts were darkened. They knew God, but they decided to turn a blind eye and mind and live their own way. Even in such an inner state of being, the mad love of God haunts us and pounds on the door of our hearts until we relent.

This is exactly what happened in my own life; in love, God haunted and hunted me down until I gave up and said you win, God. I can remember reading a similar story by Anne Lamott, who after being haunted by God one Sunday after church, felt the Holy Spirit pursuing her on the drive home. If my memory serves me correctly, she had just had an abortion and was drowning away her sorrows with alcohol. Some might rage at the fact that she had an abortion (I don't agree with it either), but this proves that whatever choices you make in life—good, bad, or indifferent—the mad love of God still haunts and pursues. What kind of God would He be if he ran because of the choices that Anne made? Of course, our sinful actions grieve the heart of God, but in His grief, He does not give up on us.

Though my own story is somewhat different than Anne's, I was a very cold-hearted and depressed young person who didn't care about anyone, even himself. People were a means to an end for me. I was a suicidal and angsty person, who truly felt as though there was no hope or point to life. When I was seventeen, on my last day of high school, looking at the overcast sky, the only thought that ran through my mind was that I wanted to die. I wasn't sure how I would go through with anything, I just knew that I wanted to go home, turn on my music, and not wake up.

God in His mad love had different plans; as I was walking out, I saw someone wearing black windbreaker pants, white sneakers, a t-shirt that had the word "revolution" on the front, and a backwards hat with dreadlocks underneath. We walked right up to each other, and the first thing I asked him was what in the world his shirt meant. He informed me that that was his church youth group. Automatically my stomach began to turn, for that was the one thing that I didn't want anything to do with. But for some reason, when He invited me, something inside me gave in and said okay. He even agreed to give me a ride to and from because I didn't drive. I don't want to bore you with a lot of the details because that is also covered in my first book, The Emotional Struggle. The fact of the matter is, by the grace of God I became a child of God. I fell deeply into His mad love. All the sadness, hopelessness, and despair that I felt melted off my hardened heart. To this day, there is no greater joy than to be Abba's child, for in this there is great joy that is ever-present even in human suffering. Beyond that, there is joy in the fact that when the Father looks upon me, He sees His radiant Son Jesus. As a result of this transformation from the inside out, I was able to stop hating myself; I was able to put down the whip, if you will. I was able to look at Him (Jesus) and find all my worth, dignity, and value in Him.

It's easy to assume that everything in my life from that point on was peachy and without toil or hardship, which is so far from the truth. The problems started when well-meaning Christians shared some testimony of how God set them free from some sort of addictive habit, and then they claimed that they never dealt with temptation or relapse ever again. Who am I to say that that can't happen? It can, but I think that for a lot of us, the Christian life is of joy and fight. We fight for joy in Christ every single day of our lives. John Piper even testifies to this reality; after the warm and fuzzy feelings go away, you tend to have a now what?

Most times in relationships, when the feelings of love and affection go away, it can be easy to be frightened and not know what to do next. Or the popular thing to do is when you no longer feel those feelings, take the easy out and leave that relationship and go after something or someone that gives you that original spark. Much of the same, I believe can be said about our walk with God. When we no longer feel the spiritual goosebumps, it can be easy to think that God has left you or forsaken you never to come back. It can be so easy to think, "I thought your love for me was so mad, God, but I don't feel it anymore!" The caution that I would implore here is to realize that the enemy can use these moments to grub ground in your soul, which is exactly why we must not rely on feelings alone, but the firm, rock steady promises of God.

I believe that a good many of us have felt that God has forsaken and abandoned us, and as such, some have metaphorically handed God divorce papers, as it were. Others of us, while we may feel abandoned or forsaken, may sit in lonely gloom or darkness, but somewhere in that darkness and gloom the promises of God still illuminate the heavy darkness with living hope. Another very quotable phrase in the Bible is, "My God, My God, why have you forsaken me?" which comes from Matthew 27:46 and Psalm 22. When we doubt the mad love of God toward us, we need not look to our emotions and feelings as our guide, but rather we must look at the weighty actions of Christ toward us.

In a broken and fallen state, none are worthy of the mad love of God. Instead because of our stiff necks and hard hearts, we all deserve eternal separation from God as result. However, there must be something much, much deeper going on that our minds and hearts simply have not realized yet. When we feel forgotten or abandoned by God, have we truly considered why Jesus felt forsaken by His Father? In the deepest sense, it was so that you and I, those who by the grace of God place their trust in Christ, may never have to be forsaken by God in the grand eternal picture. Yes, we may feel forsaken or that God does not love us madly, but in light of Christ being momentarily separated from His Father, those lies have not one hint of truth in them.

We must then allow the Holy Spirit to haunt us with this truth, for in it and because of it we have permanent and infinite access into the mad love of God. We must learn to store this truth into our memory banks because in the battle and even in the days where all seems well is when we need to remember it most.

There was a time in my life when my mind was flooded with doubt; many of my friends from college were seemingly leaving the faith, one after another. This shook my entire life like the most violent earthquake; I was unsure of what was happening and even feared for my own salvation. I choked on the words in Philippians 2:12-13, which in summary tell us to work out our salvation with fear and trembling. I began to question if I was even one of God's beloved. In popular culture, people like to say that we are all God's children, but the problem is that it fails to capture the weight that Scripture places on being a child of God. Seldom do we understand the price that Christ went through, in the name of bringing us to Himself. In Matthew 13, Jesus told the parable of the sower, which reads:

"That same day Jesus went out of the house and sat by the lake. Such large crowds gathered around him that he got into a boat and sat in it, while all the people stood on the shore. Then he told them many things in parables, saying: 'A farmer went out to sow his seed. As he was scattering the seed, some fell along the path, and the birds came and ate it up. Some fell on rocky places, where it did not have much soil. It sprang up quickly because the soil was shallow. But when the sun came up, the plants were scorched, and they withered because they had no root. Other seeds fell among thorns, which grew up and choked the plants.8 Still other seed fell on good soil, where it produced a crop – a hundred, sixty, or thirty times what was sown. Whoever has ears, let them hear'" (NIV).

This particular passage was instrumental in keeping me spiritually afloat, but that was not without months of intense sadness and depression. One of my closest friends in college had slowly been leaving the faith before my very eyes. To make matters more interesting, our families knew each other, and his mom had been praying for my salvation since I was a young boy. I never learned of that fact until I saw my friend's parents at college while at lunch. His mom came up to me, gave me a hug, got down on my level, and told me that she and her husband had been praying for my salvation since the day they met me. Though, as I said before, I had never known that fact; all I knew was that my dad taught his dad martial arts. And when I went away to college, I saw my friend practice a style of martial arts (in the chapel, of all places) that I immediately recognized. When I went up to introduce myself to him, I asked him where he had learned that style of martial arts, and he told me that his dad had taught him. When I learned of his last name and who his dad was, the dots synced in my head.

It was amazing to me; I knew that the hand of God had ordained it all. We were the best of friends and were joined by our passions for martial arts and faith. He even helped me teach my own self-defense class on campus for three years. And one day at dinner, I saw him sitting off afar in the cafeteria. So I carefully balanced the food in my lap while driving my scooter to the table. He always said he liked being by himself, but he always welcomed my company. This particular evening he looked extremely sad, like heavy rain clouds overhead. The crux of the conversation was not our usual laughter, jokes, and weird looks by others on campus. This night and many months to follow would change the trajectory of our friendship.

In the months to come, he seemed to be more to himself and even depressed, which hurt my heart as well. I didn't know what to say in response to his pain. I didn't have any answers that I thought were worthwhile to him. Frankly, they weren't, and in a lot of ways, he is far more intelligent in the areas of science and so on. All my apologetic answers merely brushed off him, which made me feel stupid compared to him, as much as I tried to understand different scientific concepts which were utterly over my head. I didn't know how to articulate what I was feeling on the inside of me. In the least dramatic sense, I felt like something in me died. Similarly, the way Jesus wept over Jerusalem is about the same way that I felt, but probably not to the same magnitude. My prayers felt powerless and even meaningless. In my own spiritual depression, God felt very distant. I felt one hundred percent out of control. Was God still in control? Was He still sovereign over everything? I didn't know if He was anymore. I would go to my apologetics class and think that it was meaningless. My apologetics professor could tell that there was something noticeably wrong; normally, I would be very talkative and ready to have a thoughtful discussion with other classmates.

One day after class, she asked me to stay behind. I waited for everyone to leave; I knew what she was going to ask me, too. As the last student left and the door shut, she walked quietly and gently over to where I was sitting. Her eyes had a look of eagerness and seriousness to them.

"Brandon, are you okay?" she asked. I couldn't keep the tears in; I started to weep right in front of her. I told her how my closest friend had left the faith and no longer believed in God. Furthermore, I confessed that I struggled to see what God was doing in all of this, why this was happening, and if my prayers even mattered. I confessed that I had my doubts that God was even real. Never in my life had I ever felt so paralyzed and alone. I told her that I simply could not know if God was still with me or exited my life altogether.

My professor then showed me this passage in Exodus 33:15, which reads, "If your Presence does not go with us, do not send us up from here" (NIV). The context here is that God's people (in the previous chapter), while Moses is with God on Mount Sinai, grow impatient and decide to make a golden calf to worship. God becomes angry (and rightfully so); He then tells Moses to leave the place they are residing, with the rest of the people. God tells Moses that His presence will be with him, but Moses is less concerned with himself than the community around him, which is why he uses the word "us." He is so desperate that he is practically pleading with God for His presence to not only be with him but with his people. I think that that is what my professor was getting at, was that she could sense my own personal desperation for the presence of God. Not only that, but I wanted my friend and others to know the mad love of God as well. But much like Moses, I wanted to know if God was pleased with me.

I know that this all might sound melodramatic to some, but as it relates to the God that haunts, when you truly have tasted the love of God, and when you have seen just how wide and deep it is, it is far more than just a subjective personal experience. Rather, you want everyone to come in contact with it, know it, and understand it. Lives are completely transformed by it, and when someone rejects it, it is not merely enough to dismiss as relativism in what one believes as truth. It is somewhat more personal than that. When one does not accept the message of the

Gospel, there should be a level of grief that comes to the heart of a Christian because when you taste it and see it and then reject it, you are rejecting the truest reality of yourself and the truest expression of love.

Many people are led to believe that their lives are their own, as though they were the captain of their own souls. But in the narrative of Scripture, we are not. Genesis 1:26 says, "Then God said, Let us make man in Our own likeness, let them have dominion over the fish of the sea, over the birds of the air, and over the cattle, over all of the earth." If we are made in God's likeness (or image), then that means that His image is on us, and He is the One to whom we should be giving our hearts and minds; but some of us have chosen to go our own way. C.S. Lewis says:

"There are only two kinds of people in the end: those who say to God, 'Thy will be done,' and those to whom God says, in the end, 'Thy will be done.' All that are in Hell, choose it. Without that self-choice, there could be no Hell. No soul that seriously and constantly desires joy will ever miss it. Those who seek find. To those who knock it is opened."

Even though the Lord's image is on us, and through that we have worth, dignity, and value, He knows that some hearts are far too stubborn to bend a knee, which is why on one hand Lewis said Thy will be done because God knew that there could be no other way. He knew that no matter what evidence or divine miracle was placed in front of some people, they would only find a way to dismiss it. That is not to say that people with that personal disposition are automatically unreachable or unredeemable; Heaven knows that as long as there is breath and a heartbeat in our bodies, there is still hope. And as Christians, prayer is our greatest weapon.

We should not give up in the spiritual fight as it relates to the eternal standing of another person. I have personally spent years of my life praying for those I love who do not know the mad love of God to fall deeply for it. There have been plenty of times when I have grown weary, wondering if God even hears me. But His love haunts me to keep praying and persevering. Sometimes I wish that God would reveal Himself to everyone and that everyone would believe in His love, but then I believe we would all truly be robots. I was listening to the lead singer of one of my favorite indie bands talk about spirituality and the hereafter. When he was asked if He believed in God and the reality of Heaven, he said that he just wasn't sure and that he didn't think that God should allow anyone to spend eternity in Hell for not knowing.

Something inside me resonated with what he was saying; part of me even wanted what he was saying to be true. But the more I read what Scripture had to say, the more I determined that it couldn't be an accurate belief. Another well-known Christian speaker once said that the love of God will eventually melt the hearts of all people. And while, again, that is an amazing thought, it doesn't align with the pages of Scripture. And, if that were the case, I don't believe that the mad love of God would haunt the hearts of people so much.

In conclusion, I think that the mad love of God haunts us all, both Christian and non, and it is up to us to make a proper response. The mad love of God haunts us on one level to respond to what we know to be true deep down inside of us. And on the other, it requires us to do something with it, i.e., to not keep it hidden, but to share it and speak of it and to let our light shine before men, for each response has its own result.

# Question for Reflection

As you've read this book, have you felt the Lord lovingly bang on the door of your heart? If so, what is causing you to resist his mad love for you?

# 24
# Anger

> "In your anger do not sin": Do not let the sun go down while you are still angry, and do not give the devil a foothold."
> Ephesians 4:26-27

IN MY PURSUIT to be more like Christ, the two things that have always tripped me up along the way are anger and lust. Sometimes in my own life, the two are not separate but go hand in hand with one another. When mentioning lust, it isn't just in terms of sexual hunger, but lust for power, money, stature, and security. A lesson that I have had to learn over and over, however painful it may be, is that nothing takes the place of the mad love of God—nothing—not family, friends, relationships, sex, money, power, authority—nothing. The Lord tells His beloved children that nothing can come before Him (Exodus 20:3-5). Why is this? In the deepest sense of the word, it is because nothing else can even come close to satisfying the deepest desire we have from within. The problem comes when we take good things and make them much bigger than they were ever intended to be. Having a beer is not bad in and of itself, but when that is your first coping mechanism or source of comfort, even that beer will become meaningless. Sometimes when I am inwardly down on myself, I am not looking deeply into the mad love of God and what He thinks of me, but, rather, hoping to drown out my sorrows with more beer and a shot of whiskey. In my estimation, this is no different than when an addict has to have a line of cocaine, or a fix of heroin to feel calm.

When we truly look at ourselves, we are all spiritual addicts in need of divine hope and recovery. I write to you as a spiritual addict and deep failure in this way. Very easily can other good things blind me from seeing and remembering that the love of God comes first and foremost in my life, which I believe is why Paul tells us to be transformed by the renewing of our minds (Romans 12:2). If this is not a daily and hourly practice for me, how quickly am I prone to seek other things for attention and a sense of satisfaction and meaning.

As I have gotten older, I find myself getting angry, agitated, and annoyed much more easily. I find myself being happy in one moment and depressed the next. I find myself becoming anxious and filled with despairing thoughts that seemly come out of thin air. The enemy attacks me in this way, suddenly and without warning. When these moments happen, it is as though I am slowly sinking in quicksand without anything to grab onto. This is when I spiral down the most; this is when the depression, sadness, and anxiety kick in with a huge wave of irrational thoughts. This only leaves me wanting to go to a remote area and scream my heart out. I know that these thoughts are not true, but then I am angry anyway because these thoughts haunt me. Most times, my prayer is that God would take me out of this world. Often, I am at war with myself because, in one layer of my life, I want to live and be like Christ, but beneath that is the frustration that I keep messing up in the process, and so it becomes easy to ask how God could love someone like that? Because if it were me, I would give that person the boot, but God isn't like that with His beloved children. I don't think that anger is an evil emotion, for, in the mad love of God, there is holy anger. It's important to know the distinction between God's anger and human anger. Scripture tells us that God is slow to anger (Psalm 103:8). He doesn't fly off the handle as we do with human anger.

Scripture also then tells us to be angry and not sin in our anger (Ephesians 4:26). That almost seems impossible, right? I know that I sin all the time in my anger, and when I am angry, I do not regard self-control or the fruit of the Spirit, which (according to Galatians 5:22-23) are: love, joy, peace, forbearance, kindness, goodness, faithfulness, gentleness and self-control. All of these are not even in my memory bank when I am taken over by anger, but the fruit of the Spirit is exactly how a child of God is supposed to act. The Bible doesn't tell us to not be angry, but if we are, it has to be in its proper time and context. As a martial arts instructor, I am always telling my students to use the skills that they know as a last resort measure. Before violence is even considered, my students are first taught to know their surroundings; are they suspicious of a certain area or person or group of people? If they are faced with a potentially violent encounter, have they done all they can to defuse the situation? Lastly, if they have exhausted their first two options, and they perceive that there are no other alternatives, it is right then to use their appropriate skills.

In the same way, when it comes to anger, have we tried to resolve an issue with the mind and heart of Christ? Have we basked in the joy of Christ to quench our anger of its desire to be made manifest? Have we let the peace of Christ rule in our hearts, knowing that He is in control? Have we allowed the peace of Christ to lead us in the way of forbearance and kindness for others, the same way that Christ leads us? Have we let the gifts of the Spirit move us to goodness, for the sake of other people? Has it caused us to remain faithful to Christ, in faith and trust? Has it allowed us to remain faithful to the vows and promises we have made to others? Have we allowed the Spirit to lead us in life and mind of self-control?

I would honestly answer no, for the vast part of my life, which grieves me and, if I am not careful, leads to inward shame and condemnation. This then leads to having to remind myself that there is no condemnation for me in Christ Jesus (Romans 8). It makes me all the more thankful for God's patience toward me, for I make mistakes and fall short of God's glory all the time. And in my mind, God is face-palming Himself, shaking His head, wondering when I'm finally going to get my poop in a group. But I don't believe that to be true, I believe that instead, His kindness and affection for me is still the same and that His face is smiling upon me.

The other day, I read a quote by Tim Keller, which said: "Salvation means much more than forgiveness. We do not simply have our slate wiped clean; we also become perfect in God's sight. And we stay perfect in God's sight. We go on as we began, having our hearts melted and molded by knowing and trusting Christ crucified." If you just read that quote, and thought, "How in the world can God see me as perfect?" I ask that question. too; if you feel utterly mind blown by that kind of mad love, you should be. If you aren't, then you need to check the spiritual temperature of your own heart. For anyone who comes into contact with the mad love of God will be forever changed and haunted by so much. It will not leave you the same. I love the words of Anne Lamott as it relates to the subject of grace:

I do not at all understand the mystery of grace, only that it meets us where we are but does not leave us where it found us.

If you struggle with anger as I do, then we must have our hearts and minds heated and melted by the love of God. For He will not relent until we see Him as He is. Furthermore, as it relates to putting my anger in a chokehold, I have found it profoundly helpful to see my life through the idea of legacy. Do I want to spend the rest of my life growing into a cranky old man, or do I want to be transformed by the love of God? I want to be transformed by the love of God. I want my future wife and children to know me for my love and not an inner grouchiness. Does that mean that my anger will vanish? No, for the old man/self will always try to rise to the surface, but when we are controlled by the Spirit and mindful of ourselves, we can quickly snuff out the temptation of the enemy.

Anger is not bad in and of itself; in some ways, it can give you the strength and drive you to need to push through a tough time in life. If I find myself angry or frustrated, I need to be wise in how I channel it and how I allow it to be in my life. I need to be sure, not to be foolish and take it out on those I love, which I have done. Foolishly. You can even use your anger in holy ways to fight back against the things that hinder you from being who you were meant to be. The anger that I am speaking of putting an end to is that which separates you from God and others. That which robs you of joy, love, peace, and affection, making you feel cold and empty on the inside. It isn't enough to just wish it away; prayer is very useful, and I highly encourage the daily practice. However, we must learn to manage our emotions through the gift of power and self-control. Anger is a human emotion that can grab hold of us all. As a man, however, I would like to speak directly to the hearts of other men, both young and old, who have a bent toward anger. Some of us express it outwardly, and with great rage. Some of us are like time bombs. And should anyone get in our crosshairs, well, then, they just happen to be the bystander who caught it. It terrifies and sickens me that I can be that way as well, but if we call ourselves men and children of God, then we must again warm our hearts in and against the pages of Scripture.

Colossians 3:19 tells us that husbands should not be harsh with their wives. I'm not a married man yet, but I do know that there are plenty of husbands in the world who are incredibly harsh with their wives, both physically and verbally. There are men in the world who only know how to blow up on their wives, worse yet, in front of their children. I'm fully aware that in the human condition, we say and do things to annoy and frustrate each other. That's only part of the game, but that does not give us as men (and as women) the right to speak rudely or harshly to each other. There are men who have raised a hand in anger to their wives (and even kids), and that is something that should not be tolerated under any circumstances. The problem is that human beings resort to fighting all the more quickly, and do not know how to talk and discuss things in a holy and Christlike manner.

The biggest downfall in all of our relationships is the sheer stubbornness of our own hearts. We would much rather be right and let our ego dominate the situation. As men, it makes far more sense to compose the self, after slamming some weights or splitting some wood with an ax, as my former psychology professor would do. But never, ever, should a man become physically violent with his wife or significant other. To cover all our bases, neither should a woman. They can be violent and abusive, too. I once had a friend whose girlfriend would be physically violent with him, and he never resisted or anything to that end. He had a hard time leaving because in his heart he loved her. I know it sounds crazy, especially from a man's perspective. And leaving abusive relationships is not as easy we make it seem. Now, if you have found yourself in the words of this chapter, I want you to know that God's mad love and grace are open to you. It can change your life; you don't have to be the person you once were; you can change by the power of His Spirit and with time.

You will have to seek the forgiveness of others to the best of your ability and be willing to accept the consequences and fallout of your actions, but that does not mean that you are somehow outside God's mad love. I know that you may experience a depth of shame and regret, but God can restore you and make you a brand-new person inside and out. The great reformers of old call it the great exchange, for when Christ was on the cross, He exchanged His righteousness for your sin and shame. I know that that might not make any logical sense to you, and in many ways, God's love is not logical by any stretch of the imagination. But I believe that our human condition needs it all the more and nonetheless.

It's in our human nature, though, to want to rebel and say NO! God can't pay for my sin and shame; I have to be the one to do that! But the fact of the matter is, there isn't enough good in the world that we can do to make right our sin. We do good things and feel better for a moment, but nothing can blot out the stain of sin the way Christ's death, burial, and resurrection can. Man-made religion says, be more, do more, work harder, show the world how badly you want to be a different and better person. But when a human being truly comes up against the grace of God, you find that all your efforts to change and not repeat the actions of old were worth nothing compared to the freedom that the grace of God provides us. The Bible says that while we were still sinners, Christ died for us (Romans 5:8). If you have found yourself living with the inner disposition of anger, it does not have to be the sum total of who you are or your true identity. When you look into the love of Christ, you will find your truest self; you will find all that you have ever longed for.

## Question for Reflection

If you can relate to me and have deep-seated anger in your life, what do you find yourself angry with? Personal choices? Things others have done to you?

# 25
# The Sudden Longing

"In a futile attempt to erase our past, we deprive the community of our healing gift. If we conceal our wounds out of fear and shame, our inner darkness can neither be illuminated nor become a light for others."

Brennan Manning

DEATH HAS BEEN PLAGUING our society more than ever through assisted suicide, which is currently legal in up to eight different states. The term "assisted suicide" is a phrase or term that should send shivers down your spine, or at least turn your stomach inside out as it does mine. Assisted suicide, however, is not something new. Its history can be traced back to the early 1900s. Much like anything in life, there are always two sides, and it's no different with the topic of assisted suicide. On the one hand, you have those who oppose it with great conviction and vigor. And on the other hand, there are those who say that it is a person's human right to choose how to leave this life.

In my own understanding, there're those living with a terminal illness, such as cancer. And then, there're those who have the never-ending thought that they want to die. To those living with a terminal illness, cancer is a horrible monster. I can remember as a kid, one of my martial arts instructors was battling a very aggressive form of brain cancer. It had apparently gone into remission. But it came back in a much more aggressive fashion. He would have to sometimes come behind the desk of our Dojo to lie down for a minute. If my memory serves me correctly, he even had a seizure. I was always amazed at how he carried himself as an instructor, in spite of that cancer that was ruining and robbing him of his life. One of my greatest memories of him was when I was in my wheelchair, and he got on my level and taught me how to throw elbows and headbutt. In my mind, I didn't know that he was dying, I thought he would be fine and live forever. Shortly after seeing him, though, my family got word that he wasn't doing well at all. His passing wrecked me as a child; that was my one experience with someone who had a terminal illness.

I remember crying heavily and feeling the frailty of human life. I knew that his body would be buried in the ground and that I would never see him again. At that age, I was taught about the reality of reincarnation, and that I might very well see him again in a different time of life. But in my young mind, I didn't know that to be true. And I still don't. But my instructor's life taught me that we are all headed to the grave in varying circumstances; it's only a matter of how you get there. He taught me that you can truly die doing what you love. I understand that every case of suffering is different, though. I have friends who joke that if they ever get to the point where they have to wear adult diapers, you should just shoot them. It seems funny in a way, but there're are people in life with severe Alzheimer's or dementia who simply do not want to be remembered in that way. A young woman by the name of Brittany had a very aggressive brain tumor. She went from having several years to live down to only a few weeks.

She didn't want to die in the ways that the doctors said cancer would take her; her family all supported her choice. She even put out a few videos on the Internet that started a huge debate; some people supported her choice, and others were appalled by it.

I obviously believe that God is the author of all life, and that life is a gift. Yet, I write these words with the utmost compassion and sincerity. We can tell someone that life is precious and that it is wrong to end their life (and it is), but we can never know the pain they are actually feeling. In the same way, we can agree that someone should die with dignity, yet we never will know what the rest of that life could have been. When we discuss the topic of death, it is my conviction that hope is the greatest and most amazing weapon. A small glimmer of hope can illuminate the darkest of circumstances. For those who profess faith and trust in Jesus Christ, He is their solid rock and greatest hope.

If I may bare my soul with you for a moment, I want to tell you that I fall within the second group of people. Those who seemingly cannot escape the thought of wanting to die. I could be having the best day, month, or what have you, and out of nowhere the thought of death will grab my attention. Oftentimes I try and shove it away somewhere in the back of my mind or cover it up with a smile. It doesn't come to my attention all the time, just at seemingly random moments of my life. When depression is deep and heavy, I often wish that God would just take me as I am sleeping. There have been nights where I have prayed that God would simply end my earthly existence, either because I was tired of my surrounding circumstances and did not feel like they would ever change, or other times I felt as though life was utterly meaningless and that my life truly never had and never would amount to anything.

Yes, even after being a Christian by the grace of God for over ten years, I still have these thoughts. Subsequently, the misconception that comes along with such confessions is one of utter confusion because Christians are meant to be happy go lucky, and have all the answers, right? This misconception stems largely from two areas of misunderstanding. One: a person simply has not read the pages of Scripture closely enough; the pages of Scripture are loaded with people who experienced depression, sorrow, and deep regret. Two: we often forget about the saints of old who struggled with depression as well. Mother Teresa struggled with her own depression and even wrote the following words:

"I want to smile even at Jesus and so hide, if possible, the pain and the darkness of my soul even from Him." I think, to a degree, it is natural in a way to hide from others. After all, the first parents, Adam and Eve, did the same in the garden. After they sinned, they discovered they were naked and covered their bodies. Thus, we humans do the exact same thing—we try and cover up our sins and mistakes; we try and hide our shame and guilt from others; and it becomes very difficult, to be honest, vulnerable, and transparent. This, I believe, based on Mother Teresa's words, was exactly what she was missing. God already knew and was deeply aware of her inward bent toward depression, sadness, and loneliness.

Consider the poetic words of Psalm 139:13-16 (NKJV):
"For You formed my inward parts;
You covered me in my mother's womb.
I will praise You, for I am fearfully and wonderfully made;
Marvelous are Your works,
And that my soul knows very well.
My frame was not hidden from You,
When I was made in secret,
And skillfully wrought in the lowest parts of the earth.
16 Your eyes saw my substance, being yet unformed.
And in Your book they all were written,
The days fashioned for me,
When as yet there were none of them."

In other words, there is nothing we can hide from God, nor should we. And I think that if Mother Teresa approached Christ with a smile on her face, and yet used that as a cover-up in His presence, He would tenderly tell her to remove the mask and unveil what is truly making her heart heavy, even though He already knows. As Christians, we are told to approach the throne of God with confidence (Hebrews 4:16). In my own words, I would write it as:

Approach the mad love of God with confidence and a shameless audacity because we don't have to hide. When you are in Christ you have constant access to His mad love, and we can approach His throne with a shameless audacity, even after we feel the guilt and shame of sin, and He will forgive us because all the wrath we deserve was poured out on the Messiah Jesus. (That does not mean, however, that we can go on living rebellious and risky lives.) The prince of preachers himself, Charles Spurgeon, was also one who wrestled with depression. In fact, he called it a soul sickness, and he also believed that the mind was just as broken as the body. He once wrote, "My spirits were sunken so low that I could weep by the hour like a child, and yet I did not know what I wept for." It's amazing that he knew and understood such a factual reality, but so many others still do not. Some even think that his depression was not a hindrance to his public ministry, but that it helped him, for he saw his depression as even something ordained by God so that he could also go and comfort another hurting soul. He clung to his faith in God, even in spite of such darkness.

I also believe that God wants us to do the same, to cling to His mad love for us and the fact that He will never let us go. And if you are not yet one who has come to know the mad love of God, I pray that this may be a means of doing so. Spurgeon even admitted to feeling ashamed for wrestling with depression as he did, but I don't believe that the shame is of God, either. Rather, the enemy attacks us with it because shame causes us to distance ourselves from God instead of drawing close to Him, which is what the enemy wants. We once again, I believe, have to come to the realization of the spiritual battle, for it is easy to pass off depression as only a physical and psychological issue. Furthermore, I believe that there is a deeply spiritual component to depression or soul sickness, as Charles Spurgeon would call it.

For in depression and soul-sickness is the longing to know that we love, belong, and are accepted far beyond a surface level. I can remember that in both of the times I was deeply suicidal, I wanted to know if there was a deeper love, knowledge, joy, and acceptance than what society had to offer. In other words, what I was looking for was the definition and embodiment of all of these things. And I found all of that in the perfection and love of Jesus Christ. The point I am intending to make here is that the Christian is far more keenly aware of their own fallen nature and need for a savior than those who only dwell on the physical. It wasn't until I was born again into the mad love of God that I realized that the entire person is broken and needs to be treated and tended to by the great doctor Himself, Jesus Christ.

I also discovered that the mad love of God was something and Someone that I could constantly go to and that His love, grace, and compassion could truly offer hope and change in the ways that I saw myself when depression struck. The mad love of God was not a construct in my mind, but a real person who understood and knew me inside and out, one whom I knew that I did not have to put on a façade for. I knew that the God-man Jesus Christ was one on whom I could rest my weary head. I love the words in Isaiah 9:2:

"The people walking in darkness have seen a great light; on those living in the land of deep darkness light has dawned" (NIV). Christ is the ever-present light out of the darkness that never dims or fades out. The mad love of God can restore the broken mind and soul in ways medicine and counseling cannot, though I am not opposed to either of those pathways, as I believe they are God's common grace to all. God can use those as a means to one's healing, but in the truest sense, the healing we all seek is found in nothing but the mad love of God and our identity in Him.

Identity in Christ is so very crucial to our survival, for the consequences of not knowing our identity are intensely serious. Once we forget who we truly are and where our value lies, our emotions will start to take control, and we will spiral deeper into sorrow. I know this all too well in my own life. For, when I take my eyes off Christ, I am pulled more deeply into inner shame and regret. When this happens, I am more prone to think that God is against me rather than for me. It's more believable that God hates me rather than loves me. The fact of the matter, and what many tend to forget, is that when a person is in Christ, it does not matter what we think, but what He thinks.

I feel like I am worthless and have no purpose, but the mad love of the Father has blessed me with infinite worth and immense purpose in life. Christ is the truest way to escape my entrapped mind. Philosophy suggests that we are what we think and feel, but my thoughts and emotions are often fleeting and ever-changing. And yet Christ's affection and love for me are ever constant and do not change. Religion will tell us to go into ourselves and to change how we think by our own power. The depressed person does not need to go any deeper into themselves, but they need to be rescued from the pit that is themselves. Christ is and was the only way for me to have solace from the thought of wanting to die. As I said earlier on, some days the thought of wanting to die, or not wanting to be in this body anymore seems appealing. There are some days when I am far too aware of not only my own brokenness but that of the world around me. And so being with Christ in utter perfection and glory is my ultimate desire. In a way, the Apostle Paul faced this very perplexity himself. In Philippians 1:21 Paul writes the words, "For me to live is Christ, and to die is gain" (ESV). While there is no clear indication that Paul was in fact suicidal, we can know that he endured a hard life as Christ's apostle. He details his suffering in 2 Corinthians 11:16-27:

"But whatever anyone else dares to boast of—I am speaking as a fool—I also dare to boast of that. Are they Hebrews? So am I. Are they Israelites? So am I. Are they offspring of Abraham? So am I. Are they servants of Christ? I am a better one—I am talking like a madman—with far greater labors, far more imprisonments, with countless beatings, and often near death. Five times I received at the hands of the Jews the forty lashes less one. Three times I was beaten with rods. Once I was stoned. Three times I was shipwrecked; for a night and a day I was adrift at sea; on frequent journeys, in danger from rivers, danger from robbers, danger from my own people, danger from Gentiles, danger in the city, danger in the wilderness, danger at sea, danger from false brothers; in toil and hardship, through many a sleepless night, in hunger and thirst, often without food, in cold and exposure" (ESV).

Again, it's not clear by any means that Paul was actually suicidal, but I believe that it is fairly safe to say that he might have been feeling a bit weary in his heart and mind and longed for the perfect presence of Christ. The point is that he faced that perplexity and chose to continue on the mission that God had given him for the sake of others (Philippians 1:24-26). In my own life, my prayer has been that God might remove the thought of wanting to die from my mind and that those moments wouldn't return. But in the same way, Paul asked Jesus to remove the thorn from his side:

"But he said to me, 'My grace is sufficient for you, for my power is made perfect in weakness.' Therefore I will boast all the more gladly about my weaknesses, so that Christ's power may rest on me. 10 That is why, for Christ's sake, I delight in weaknesses, in insults, in hardships, in persecutions, in difficulties. For when I am weak, then I am strong" (2 Corinthians 12:9-10, ESV).

In this passage, Jesus is giving Paul something much greater than physical healing, He (Jesus) is giving Paul Himself; He is giving Paul the embodiment of grace. Because Paul has Christ Himself, he has a radical change in his outlook on life. Instead of letting his inward weariness get the upper hand, he allows the power of Christ to compel him into a stronger and bolder outlook on his life. Christ can do the same, not only for myself but also for others. Paul wanted Christ to be glorified both in his earthly life and his death, and the simple beauty of that statement is that it can truly change how you live and how you view your life.

Even with having cerebral palsy, I know that people are watching me on a daily basis, and so I pray that my life can reflect hope and God's glory, regardless of how I am feeling in my body or my mind. I have heard many followers of Christ pray that they might suffer and even die well. Some might look at that particular view of suffering and death as grim and even disgusting, but I find it to be a very courageous one. Some days, my only prayer is that God will grant me the strength to get out of bed, and when I am experiencing deep depression or anxiety or both, that He would grant me the ability to hold onto Him and that He would hold onto me and pull me through the darkness. In this sense, we really can do all things through Christ who strengthens me-you-us (Philippians 4:13).

Athletes take this verse out of context all the time, but Paul was talking about something much deeper. He is speaking of being content in Christ; he is pointing toward the reality that in whatever circumstance, in death or life and in hope or despair, He is strengthened by the power of Christ, not only to live but to act in a manner worthy of Christ. The doctrine of the perseverance of the saints has been a deep comfort, both as a follower of Christ and one who suffers from depression. Simply put, it is God and His mad love that carries us to the end of our faith journey. It is not us or our strength that makes it to the end, but it has everything to do with the amazing faithfulness of God the Father.

Consider the words in Philippians 1:6, "And I am sure of this, that he who began a good work in you will bring it to completion at the day of Jesus Christ" (ESV). The doctrine of the perseverance of the saints (or preservation of the saints) is in some ways a double-edged sword. On one side of the sword, it cuts and slashes away at our pride, and on the other side, it is a bold confirmation that God will never give up on His beloved. You may be a Christian and feel that you haven't made any progress spiritually or in any other area of your life. You may feel like the most worthless Christian ever and that God should not bother with you any longer. But that is a lie from the enemy's mouth. The only option we have, then, is to let the Spirit of God work away in our lives in every area. Especially in the mind, you may wrestle with depression in various ways for the rest of your human existence, but you can rest deeply on God's faithfulness, that He will lead you through all the fog and dark valleys of the soul. God is not burned by the depression that is present in your life, He's not powerless over it, nor is He confused about what to do with it. I believe that in many ways, He may be using the heaviness of our hearts and darkness of our minds to bring us to Himself. We don't have to have it all together; you don't have to act as if everything is okay; you don't have to live every day with a fake smile upon your face.

In Christ we are free to cry out to Him with all our hearts; we are free to bang on God's door until it opens. C.S. Lewis, in his book *A Grief Observed*, said in regard to knocking on God's door:

"'Knock and it shall be opened.' But does knocking mean hammering and kicking the door like a maniac?" Even he understood the frustration of having to deal with deep grief and feeling as though he was left alone. Sometimes it feels as though we have to be left to wander in the desert by ourselves, and so we are left to scream and hope that Heaven hears us. I believe that, in truth, we don't have to kick at God's door like a maniac, for His love and presence are always with us. But when the road is long and frustrating, I truly believe that He understands and even welcomes us to be maniacs at times because He likes the intimacy with His children. It is no different than when a child swings away in their parent's arms because they feel abandoned or that a promise is broken; the parent simply holds onto their child while they cry and flail.

I can't tell you enough how important it is to know that God loves you. There is not a greater truth in the entire universe. He loves you, and I believe that the mad love of God is trying to get the attention of countless people every day, including you and even me sometimes to this very day. You're not too much of a mess for God's love. It doesn't matter what your past or present circumstances are; there is nothing that the mad love of God cannot make new. There is no hole deep enough that God cannot rescue you from it; you have not run so far off that God has lost you. Consider the parable of the lost sheep:

"So he told them this parable: 'What man of you, having a hundred sheep, if he has lost one of them, does not leave the ninety-nine in the open country, and go after the one that is lost, until he finds it? And when he has found it, he lays it on his shoulders, rejoicing. And when he comes home, he calls together his friends and his neighbors, saying to them, 'Rejoice with me, for I have found my sheep that was lost.' Just so, I tell you, there will be more joy in Heaven over one sinner who repents than over ninety-nine righteous persons who need no repentance'" (Luke 15:4-7, ESV).

Jesus does not lose sight of His beloved, and He will not lose sight of you.

## Question for Reflection

As described in 1 Kings 19:1-14, random, heavily dark thoughts are common in modern Christians and biblical figures. As you engage with the passage, ask yourself: Do you see how the Lord takes care of him even in a severely depressed state? How can you seek his own loving-kindness in your own darkness?

# 26
# His Grace

"God's grace is so powerful that it has the capacity to overcome natural resistance to it."
R.C. Sproul

GOD'S GRACE IS the single greatest gift in my life and probably the entire universe. It's not something I can simply stop talking about. In fact, it's something that has to be talked about and read about over and over. For one does not simply outgrow the grace of God or have such a profound understanding of it that they no longer have to meditate on it or dwell in its presence. No, the grace of God is something that is wrapped in the mad love of God that permeates the life of a Christian. The grace of Jesus Christ has truly wrecked my life in the best way possible; it has not only changed how I view myself but also others around me, though I did my best to evade it for the longest time. In the Reformed/Protestant camp, there is a doctrine called Irresistible Grace, which is again a doctrine that God has truly used to change my life. The misconception is that you can't resist God's grace at all; you can. C.S. Lewis is a prime example of wanting nothing to do with God or Christianity as a whole, but the Spirit of God changed the very inclination of his heart.

"You must picture me alone in that room in Magdalen, night after night, feeling, whenever my mind lifted even for a second from my work, the steady, unrelenting approach of Him whom I so earnestly desired not to meet. That which I greatly feared had at last come upon me. In the Trinity Term of 1929, I gave in, and admitted that God was God, and knelt and prayed: perhaps, that night, the most dejected and reluctant convert in all England. I did not then see what the most shining and obvious thing is now; the Divine humility that will accept a convert even on such terms. The Prodigal Son at least walked home on his own feet. But who can duly adore that Love which will open the high gates to a prodigal who is brought in kicking, struggling, resentful, and darting his eyes in every direction for a chance of escape? The words 'compelle intrare,' compel them to come in, have been so abused by wicked men that we shudder at them; but, properly understood, they plumb the depth of the Divine mercy. The hardness of God is kinder than the softness of men, and His compulsion is our liberation."

I love the way Lewis describes his conversion experience: "the steady, unrelenting approach of Him whom I so earnestly desired not to meet. That which I greatly feared had at last come upon me." Lewis earnestly desired not to meet the living God. And if I had been Lewis, I would have said to this pestering presence: "Are you mad? Can't you leave me alone and bother someone else?" Lewis says that he was the prodigal son that was "brought in kicking, struggling, resentful, and darting his eyes in every direction for a chance to escape." R.C. Sproul may, in fact, take a slightly different view, but I think that in some ways they complement each other:

It is not that the Holy Spirit drags people kicking and screaming to Christ against their wills. The Holy Spirit changes the inclination and disposition of our wills, so that whereas we were previously unwilling to embrace Christ, now we are willing, and more than willing. Indeed, we aren't dragged to Christ; we run to Christ, and we embrace Him joyfully because the Spirit has changed our hearts. So while Sproul may have disagreed with the language Lewis used to describe his conversion, I do believe that the Holy Spirit worked on the heart of Lewis over time and thus changed the inclination of his heart, allowing Lewis to be not simply willing to bend a knee to Christ but to take off running toward

Him. The fact of the matter is that the grace (love and mercy of God) changed Lewis's life in a way that nothing else in this world could. The mad love of God is not simply love; it is grace, mercy, and truth all wrapped up into one. In John Chapter 4, the Samaritan woman has her life changed by the grace of God when she discovers that Jesus Christ is the living water that her soul is longing for. After she has this life-changing encounter with Christ, she hurries off to go tell everyone that she comes in contact with who she just encountered. This is the mark of a changed life due to the grace of God. I want to tell you again that there is nothing more vital and important than the grace of God. There is nothing more valuable and sustaining than the grace of God. And all the things that we believe place such value and esteem on our lives simply do not measure up. Consider the words of the Apostle Paul in Philippians 3:8-10:

"Indeed, I count everything as loss because of the surpassing worth of knowing Christ Jesus my Lord. For his sake I have suffered the loss of all things and count them as rubbish, in order that I may gain Christ and be found in him, not having a righteousness of my own that comes from the law, but that which comes through faith in Christ, the righteousness from God that depends on faith—that I may know him and the power of his resurrection, and may share his sufferings, becoming like him in his death" (ESV).

Paul was another person whose life was changed by the grace of God, He was a persecutor of Christians, and, like Lewis, did not want anything to do with how the mission of Christ was changing the lives of so many people. And as much as I believe in what R.C. Sproul has to say about changing the inclinations of one's heart and not dragging us kicking and screaming, the grace of God did knock the Apostle Paul on his backside quite literally (Acts 9). From there on his life was changed in a very dramatic fashion. He went on to write a huge chunk of the New Testament. How could this possibly happen, if not for a divine miracle? It can't. To my knowledge, I have never known anyone that wakes up in the morning and says to themselves, "I think I want to be a Christian today!" That simply does not happen, unless there is first the work of God's grace. I know what I'm saying is filled with controversy, for people like to assume that they made the choice in and of themselves to choose Christ. Grace finds us; the mad love of God finds us.

Grace is not something that is of itself comfortable. C.S. Lewis made the following statement on religion: "I didn't go to religion to make me happy. I always knew a bottle of Port would do that. If you want a religion to make you feel really comfortable, I certainly don't recommend Christianity."

Many seem to go to religion for the peace and comfort that it can and does offer. But there is a much deeper reality to it. Grace confronts the self; it confronts everything that we keep stowed away so tightly in our hearts, and it confronts what we perceive about ourselves and others in our minds. Lewis also says that God cannot give us peace apart from Himself. And if that is the case, He wants to radically change you from the inside out. Nothing else in human history will confront our very personhood the way that the grace of Jesus Christ does. Nothing will confront our pride, our stubbornness, our envy, our greed, or our lust the way His grace does.

When you first come up against His grace, you will quickly realize that you have been taken off the throne of your own life. It is no longer you or I that is king, but He is. Or, as the Apostle Paul would say: it is no longer I who live, but Christ who lives in me (Galatians 2:20). By His grace the entire scope of your life changes; you go from having a deep sense of self, to having a deeper sense of what He wants. Which begs the question: What does He want? In the greatest sense of the word, He wants you, all of you. Not so much your money, status, reputation, or anything that we hold with great esteem. He just wants you. Once again, going back to the words of Mr. Lewis:

"Give me all of you!!! I don't want so much of your time, so much of your talents and money, and so much of your work. I want YOU!!!

ALL OF YOU!! I have not come to torment or frustrate the natural man or woman, but to KILL IT! No half measures will do. I don't want to only prune a branch here and a branch there; rather I want the whole tree out! Hand it over to me, the whole outfit, all of your desires, all of your wants and wishes and dreams. Turn them ALL over to me, give yourself to me and I will make of you a new self---in my image. Give me yourself and in exchange, I will give you Myself. My will shall become your will. My heart shall become your heart."

I believe that Lewis is right in his description of how much God just wants us, and only us. But why does He want us? That is a whole other question altogether. God obviously does not need anything or anyone, but the beauty of it all is that even the Trinity is a communal expression of love (mad love), and that love is expressed in the Father sending His Son Jesus to live among us, teach us, and ultimately suffer for our sins and rise again, so that we may be with Him in eternity. It's as though the mad love of God unfolded a story in which we were the characters that reveal His glory, which is in itself an act of sheer grace. The push back becomes, why would God want me? I'm too broken, have made too many mistakes, have too many addictions and insecurities! I barely do anything right!

You, my friend, are the exact kind of person that needs His grace. Because you already know that you're a mess. And when you come face to face with His grace, you don't turn your eyes away from it and you don't scoff at it. You instead embrace it with open arms, as opposed to the person who says no to His grace over and over again. This isn't to say that God can't break through the cold stoniness of a heart; we have clearly seen that He can. However, I believe that the mad love of God is after those whom He knows will receive His grace (the elect if you will).

I used to think that I couldn't be an instrument or soldier in God's kingdom because of how my body was. How could I be used mightily for His glory and kingdom if I could barely use the right side of my body and have so much shame over it? Man, did I have it wrong! I finally realized that in spite of having cerebral palsy, God's grace and glory were shown mightily through me when I allowed Him to use me. What I began to see was how God could use my own life story, be it to simply inspire others or, even better, to bring them into a relationship with God Himself. I could use all the pain and suffering in my life, by God's grace, to help others see the goodness and mercy of God in my life. Slowly but surely, as God's grace has transformed my own life, I have noticed a boldness in myself and a change in my demeanor.

I noticed in myself that I went from believing, "I can't do that," to "I can do that," and not in a cocky or arrogant sort of way. It wasn't that I thought that I could be a professional football player, but when you go from people telling you as a kid that you aren't smart enough to go to college, and you end up graduating college with honors, you can only credit that to God's love and grace toward you. The grace of God can be the single greatest weapon against shame, regret, and self-pity. Sometimes, they will rear their ugly heads, but God will help you to remember who you are in His sight. If it weren't for the grace of God, I'm not sure where I would be in my life right now. I honestly even hesitate to think about it, but I know that His grace has brought me to where I am in my life now, and I pray that His mad love and grace will open up your entire person to His glory.

## Question for Reflection

Have you truly allowed God's grace to change you inside and out? Or is it an abstract concept to you?

# 27
# For the Outcast

> "God chose what is low and despised in the world, even things that are not, to bring to nothing things that are, so that no human being might boast in the presence of God. And because of him you are in Christ Jesus, who became to us wisdom from God, righteousness and sanctification and redemption, so that, as it is written, 'Let the one who boasts, boast in the Lord'"
> 1 Corinthians 1:28-31 (ESV)

IN THE LAST CHAPTER, I mentioned briefly the fact that having cerebral palsy blinded me from seeing that I could be a mighty warrior in God's kingdom. It occurred to me moments after finishing the previous chapter that it might be good to expand on the topic, as there are many physically challenged people in the world who might not know the mad love of God. I love the parable of the great banquet in Luke Chapter 14. Jesus says, "He said to the man who had invited him, 'When you give a dinner or a banquet, do not invite your friends or your brothers or your relatives or rich neighbors, lest they also invite you in return and you be repaid. But when you give a feast, invite the poor, the crippled, the lame, the blind, and you will be blessed because they cannot repay you. For you will be repaid at the resurrection of the just'" (ESV).

When it comes to speaking of Jesus, one of the things that I love speaking about the most is His compassion for physically challenged people. He did not turn away from them; he did not act as if they did not exist, and He wasn't burdened by them. He wasn't afraid to be in close proximity with them and even be in intimate contact (touch) with them. For example, in Mark 1 He touches and heals a man with leprosy. In those days, those with leprosy were seen as untouchable; they were seen as outcasts. In my own research on the condition, I discovered that

## For the Outcast

those who had contracted the disease were often fired from their job and lost connection with family, friends, and close human contact overall. Putting myself in the place of someone who has (or had) leprosy, I cannot imagine how deeply lonely a person could become, as they were isolated from community.

I could only imagine how much they longed for a simple touch from someone, or even the amount of shame or disgust that they had when looking at their bodies decaying before their very eyes. Even though leprosy is curable by today's standards, it is vital to know Christ's compassion for those who feel like social outcasts. For Jesus, I can easily see that He has no hesitation in reaching out and touching those who are diseased; He doesn't think that He might get the disease; He doesn't look at them as disgusting or gross.

What must it have been like for someone with leprosy to have the Son of God touch them without hesitation or caution? Think about what they must have felt like as His radiant touch not only touched the surface of their skin but also moved through their entire body! I'll bet their lives were never the same, nor were they immediately recognizable when they returned to seemingly normal society. I don't know if all the healings that Christ performed led to a cognitive understanding of who He was, in the sense of salvation. But it would be very hard for me to think that all the people that Christ healed were ever the same again. Since Jesus had the authority to heal all people of all afflictions, He was not limited by touch, as He could simply speak, and a person would be healed. For instance, in Matthew 9, He heals a paralyzed man simply by saying, "Take heart, my son, your sins are forgiven." Even though He did not touch this man, His words are still deeply personal, as He calls the man "my son" and professes to the man that his sins are forgiven. (More on that aspect later.) Another healing that grabs my attention is in Mark Chapter 8, which tells us that a group of people brought a visually impaired man to Jesus, whom they begged Him to touch. And then the text tells us that Jesus took the man by the hand. I love that phrase. I love that Jesus actually holds this person's hand.

Again, think about what that must be like, for the Son of God to be holding your hand! Then Jesus spits on his eyes and lays His hands on him. He spits on the man… I never would have thought that God would send His Son down to earth to rub His spit in one's eyes, in the name of healing. Jesus asks him, "Do you see anything?" And the man replies: "I see people, but they look like trees walking." Then Jesus touches him again, and he sees everything clearly. It doesn't get more personal than Jesus spitting on a person in the name of healing unless you're a deaf man, and He (Jesus) sticks His own fingers in your ears (Mark 7). Hopefully, the man's ears were clean, but even if they weren't, that still wouldn't have kept Jesus away from him. And in that way, I don't think anything should keep us away (as Christians) from people who are outwardly different than us in physical appearance or ability, though I am not naïve to the reality that being around the physically challenged for some is very difficult. John Piper tells people in his congregation to actually see the disability, not look away from it. To see the way Jesus saw.

John Piper hints at Luke 18:35-43, in which there is a visually impaired man who was a homeless man and a beggar. The passage does not indicate how long this man had been a beggar or how he got to be this way. All we know, and all we can speculate, is that he had been that way for a while. But he can hear footsteps passing by his location; he asks what is happening, and people tell him that Jesus of Nazareth is passing by. In an instant, he cries out, "Jesus, Son of David, have mercy on me!" The passage tells us that the people in front of Jesus rebuked him. They probably told him to be quiet, not to make a scene, and not to disturb Jesus. Yet, this man is desperate, and he refuses to keep silent; he has the shameless audacity to cry out to Jesus a second time; he simply does not care if he is causing a scene or if he is even disturbing Jesus. Jesus' response is different than the people in front of Him. In fact, He demands that this man be brought to Him. Jesus gets personal with this man, even though He probably already knew where this man was sitting and that he would cry out to Him. He asks, "What do you want me to do for you?" The man replies (and probably with great desperation), "Lord, let me recover my sight."

Jesus responds to him, "Recover your sight; your faith has made you well." The passage goes on to tell us that the man recovered his sight immediately and followed Jesus, glorifying God. Once again, it is noteworthy how the people with Jesus tried to silence the man, but Jesus responds differently and with compassion. I think that in some ways, in our churches today, we care more about the appearance and flawless execution of our church services than about the presence of a mentally handicapped person who appears distracting to our precious church service. That's the problem though, right? What if, then, we saw these amazing humans as less of a distraction and more of a reflection of God's love and glory? What if the body of Christ moved toward them and their families more, instead of caring about the outward appearance of how our church services look?

The body of Christ, the Church, should be the most compassionate people group to the physically challenged community because it's painfully obvious how Christ cares for those who cannot walk, who are deaf, who cannot speak, and who cannot see. So why aren't we? Why don't more churches have more opportunities for physically challenged people to be more involved in the body of Christ? Or offer various outreaches and ministries specifically for them? I'm not saying that all churches are like this, but in my own experience I am almost always the only one with cerebral palsy or the only one who has an outward and apparent physical condition. Not to sound dramatic, but the odds of not being the only physically challenged person in church on a Sunday is one out of a hundred. That doesn't mean that I have always been the only one, but the odds are still very rare.

In my experience, any ministry for the deaf that a church has eventually goes away. And any mentally handicapped person that I have ever seen in a church service has eventually disappeared. I am aware that this is a very complex and multifaceted issue, but ultimately it is an area in which the body of Christ can improve by leaps and bounds. I truly believe that this is, indeed, the heart of Christ, as well. He wants physically challenged people to know of His mad love also. He wants them to know that their sin is forgiven the same way He proclaimed to the paralytic in Matthew 9. I think that is something able-bodied people forget as well. We can get so caught up in seeing physically challenged people as inspirational and someone special that it can be easy to mask the fact that those of us with these challenges are just as broken and sinful as the next person.

Broken and sinful in the sense of the inner disposition, not the exterior, meaning that it wasn't because of their sin or the sin of anyone else that they were born in such a way. The warming words of amazing grace extend even to them.

Amazing grace,

How sweet the sound

That saved a wretch like me.

Heaven knows that before my conversion, I was a wretch, not living for anything more than myself and living with no higher purpose or calling. My heart aches for more people like me to know that love. It can also be very hard for a lot of people who are physically challenged to even get to church on Sunday. Location and transportation are factors as well. Even though we live in a time when sermons are a click away, it is the community factor that is the most vital factor in the life of every human being. Sometimes we don't see them, simply because there is no means through which they can be seen. I think that as the body of Christ, when we know that factor, it is all the more important to be present with the light of Christ, to be thoughtful in our interactions with those who may not have access to constant streams of physical community.

In today's context, people with physical challenges (and non) can connect with each other at a moment's notice. With this reality, it is possible for people to connect with others that not only have physical challenges but share the same faith as well. I have done this myself. And for some, this is the only sense of connection that they have. Some don't have homes that are easy to get in and out of on their own. Transportation is another factor, as well, for me; I don't drive a car of my own, largely because of my own startle reflexes at loud sudden noises. Yes, there are driving adaptions and transportation services. But time and location also play a part. It is safe to say then, that a vast majority of physically challenged people long for the same community, intimacy, and sense of belonging that we all do and that we take for granted on a daily basis.

Sometimes for me, all I can do is sit in my room, pray, read the Bible, journal, and listen to sermons. All these things are well and good, and I know that the Lord's presence is with me wherever I go. It still does not remove the reality of the fact that the soul gets lonely and even aches at times for a moment of love, embrace, and affection. Some of us don't have immediate access to friends; life gets busy for people, and sometimes it's truly hard to come by friends who actually care and are not the fair-weather type of person. I, for one, have a very small circle of friends. I don't see them as much as I'd like, but when I do see them, my inner disposition tends to rise to a more hopeful outlook. Good friends, however, are extremely difficult to come by. I personally have had to sift through numerous people who only reached out to me or spent time with me when it benefited them.

It was an extremely painful and lonely time for me, but when I began to realize my own worth and value, I began to not tolerate being treated certain ways. It's not unloving or un-Christlike to sever ties or relationships with people who are unhealthy. It's not unloving or un-

Christlike to put boundaries or barriers up with people who do not reciprocate the same love and care as you give them. If you are one who finds themselves stuck in the confines of your room, lack transportation, or don't have a lot of friends or a church community, I want you to know a few things:

1) God loves you, so very madly and deeply. You are not a mistake, nor did He not know what He was doing when He formed you. He is for you, and He has a purpose for you and things that He wants you to do with your life. He has gifted you in ways that you can share with the world around you and glorify Him with. He loves you from head to toe. He knows the pain and loneliness that you feel in your soul. He knows when you lay your head down and when you wake. He will love you in ways you have always wanted, and He will love you even when you don't have a love for yourself.

2) If you find yourself reading this and you feel His Spirit moving in your mind and heart, don't fight it; let His love in. Let His love break through the stubbornness and hardness of heart. Come before Him with an honest heart; lay all your sin, shame, and guilt before Him. Let Him cleanse you and make you a new creation from the inside out. It is far better to spend the days of your life in His love and presence than to die apart from His love and be forever trapped in yourself.

3) Your identity is found in Christ and Christ alone; nothing comes before that, for that is your true self. Scripture tells us that we are hidden with Christ (Colossians 3:1-4). Nothing else defines you, not your physical condition or appearance; what defines you first and foremost is the mad love of God. The biggest mental and emotional trap we can fall into is when we start to believe that, "I am my disability. I am my condition or sickness." Yes, you may live with it, and it makes up a part of who you are, but overall it is not the sum total of who you are. In this world, you will find people who won't understand or even accept you, but try not to internalize that, for not even their acceptance or embrace

of you affects you. You might long for relational love, dating, and even a marriage someday with a man or woman, and you may feel like that may not be possible because of how you are. You may feel like you wouldn't want to burden others with needing help or ask someone to take care of you. You are not a burden; you are a blessing and a gift. And if you long for that type of relational intimacy, I highly suggest knowing who you are in Christ first and foremost and being comfortable in your own skin. For no one will love you as perfectly as you desire, and no one will love you as perfectly as Christ has and will continue to.

## Question for Reflection

As I mentioned in the chapter, having cerebral palsy at some points in my life has made me feel like an outcast. Have you ever felt like an outcast, even when going to church?

# 28
# Seeing the Glory

"As he passed by, he saw a man blind from birth. And his disciples asked him, 'Rabbi, who sinned, this man or his parents, that he was born blind?' Jesus answered, 'It was not that this man sinned, or his parents, but that the works of God might be displayed in him. We must work the works of him who sent me while it is day; night is coming, when no one can work. As long as I am in the world, I am the light of the world.' Having said these things, he spit on the ground and made mud with the saliva. Then he anointed the man's eyes with the mud and said to him, 'Go, wash in the pool of Siloam' (which means Sent). So he went and washed and came back seeing."
John 9:1-6 (ESV)

SOME YEARS AGO, prominent atheist Richard Dawkins broke the internet with a social media post regarding fetuses that have Down Syndrome. In short, he said that they should be aborted and that a woman trying to get pregnant should simply try again. As you could imagine, pro-life advocates went on the attack to defend the reality that children born with Down Syndrome are actually a gift and make life better for others. After I read Dawkins's remarks on abortion and how it is, in his eyes, immoral not to abort such a life, I felt a deep sickness in my stomach, as though I could feel to a degree the heart and Spirit of God aching inside my own chest. Even now, as I write these words, the same ache is still active inside me. As I tried to portray in the last chapter, the mad love of God extends even to those who are physically challenged and broken in spirit. In the parable of the great banquet, Jesus had invited a few people who appeared to have nothing wrong with them physically, but there was everything wrong with them spiritually speaking. They all made excuses as to why they couldn't come. In the following verses, Jesus teaches the parable of the great banquet:

"'Go out quickly to the streets and lanes of the city, and bring in the poor and crippled and blind and lame.' And the servant said, 'Sir, what you commanded has been done, and still there is room.' And the master said to the servant, 'Go out to the highways and hedges and compel people to come in, that my house may be filled. For I tell you, none of those men who were invited shall taste my banquet'" (ESV).

What is going on here? I believe that Jesus is trying to point to the human condition. He is showing us that we can become so wrapped up in the affairs of life that we forget the most important moment in our daily rhythms, which is to show up to God's great banquet so that we can become full of Him. I also believe that is what 1 Corinthians 1:28-31 is portraying as well:

"God chose what is low and despised in the world, even things that are not, to bring to nothing things that are, so that no human being might boast in the presence of God. And because of him you are in Christ Jesus, who became to us wisdom from God, righteousness and sanctification and redemption, so that, as it is written, 'Let the one who boasts, boast in the Lord'" (ESV). Some people are far too puffed up and full of themselves to see their need for forgiveness and grace, too full of themselves to know and understand that the mad love of God is what they need, so God chooses what is low and despised to reveal His character, mad love, and glory. Low and despised are not words that we should be repelled by, but instead, plunge ourselves into.

You may be a physically challenged person and feel you don't have much to offer to the world or that you are not very smart, an outcast, or that no one will ever love you. His love is for you, and His love can lift you up from the deepest and darkest pit. His glory can radiate through you, even as you wake in the morning and a smile breaks upon your face. You may be a parent, biologically speaking or otherwise, who takes care of one or more special needs children. I would venture to say that sometimes you can feel your spirit growing faint or weary. His love and

Spirit can renew your strength, He can provide you with all you need to be the light of Christ to those He has graciously placed in your care.

You may feel like what you are doing is insignificant, but I can truly tell you, that at the end of your life, the Father will embrace you and say, "Well done, my good and faithful servant. I truly believe that special needs people can reveal God's glory in a way that most others cannot. That isn't to say that no one else is of value or great worth because of Christ, but that to some degree some special needs people can be more open to the message of the Gospel.

Earlier this year, there was a Catholic group in Mexico reenacting the crucifixion of Christ. As the actor who was portraying Christ was carrying the cross on his back, a young boy with Down Syndrome came up beside him and wrapped him in a hug. What shameless audacity this young boy had to simply run up to the person acting like Jesus and wrap his arms around the imitation of Christ. I wonder if that should not be our own heart posture to the mad love of the Father, directly shown to us by His beloved Son Jesus on the cross. What if we all were like this young boy and ran to Christ without fear of rejection, ridicule, insecurity, shame, guilt, regret, or self-hatred.

What if we ran to Him, knowing that He longs to embrace us as well? What if there was not a single ounce of shame in saying that we know Him and that we are His? Peter denied Christ three times (Luke 22:54-62), and some Christians today shrink back at mentioning the name of Christ because we fear that the more sophisticated people of society will scoff at us and call us dumb for holding such a belief. Yet, I wonder if this young boy's actions speak more to the love of God working inside him and the glory of God that we can see bursting out of him. Did this young boy fully comprehend the love of God and what the message of the cross is? I believe so, though he may have not known it in a deep doctrinal way. I do believe that we can see the glory of God radiating through this young boy's demeanor.

Any person that I have ever met with Down Syndrome has had the most radiant smile, and I cannot help but see the glory of God in each of them. It is important that the church and Christians at large be more inclusive of those who have Down Syndrome, as well as communicating God's love to them in a way that they can understand on their own terms. The same can be said about a young man who was raised in a Christian home and just happens to have Down Syndrome. He says: "Because of Jesus I have a servant's heart." There was a moment in Ryan's life when he asked Jesus to be his Savior, and with the servant's heart that God bestowed upon him, God had it planned for him and his family to travel to Peru. His mom was a nurse practitioner who worked with special needs children. In the story that I watched about Ryan's testimony, they weren't sure how Ryan would handle travel and thought that maybe he would get tired or become irritable, but God's hand was not only on Ryan but also on the rest of his family.

When they went on the mission trip, his family said that Ryan and his beaming smile set the tone for the entire trip. The greatest part was when they got to spend time at a special needs school. Ryan's mom was scheduled to give a talk but first wanted Ryan to read his testimony to everyone in attendance. Apparently, some of the staff were blown away by his ability to read. Ryan knew and understood that he was different from the rest of society in some ways. He seemed very secure in himself in that way. What hit me the most about his testimony was that he said we all need God. The sound of his voice was filled with such assurance of that reality.

I have no doubt in my mind that God is using Ryan's story to touch the hearts and minds of people around him. But even more so, others like him. It's very clear that his need and love for God is not foolishness to him; rather, it is his deepest need and sense of peace and joy. Scripture tells us that the message of the cross is foolishness to those who are perishing (1 Corinthians 1:18). Foolishness and complete nonsense to believe that one man claimed to be the Son of God and died for the sins of humanity. Foolishness to believe in such a fairytale, but Jesus says in response to those who think the message of the cross is foolish:

"And calling to him a child, he put him in the midst of them 3 and said, 'Truly, I say to you, unless you turn and become like children, you will never enter the kingdom of Heaven. Whoever humbles himself like this child is the greatest in the kingdom of Heaven.'" (Matthew 18:2-4, ESV). His disciples were asking Jesus who the greatest would be in Heaven, and it's apparent they were missing the point entirely. Jesus was saying to them that when you let go of your pride, your ego, and your ability to know all the answers, you are more open to humbly and gratefully accept the invitation into the kingdom of God.

We are more willing to run up to Jesus joyfully as the previously mentioned boy with Down Syndrome did, and wrap our arms around Christ. I truly believe that people with Down Syndrome and even those who are severely mentally handicapped are created so that we can see His glory. Even if a person cannot fully comprehend the message of the Gospel and has to depend on the care of others for the rest of his or her life, they are still a beautiful blessing to the world, made in the image of God. Some time ago, I read a story about a family who adopted a young woman who was severely mentally handicapped. She required much care from the family that opened their home to her. And the only thing they could keep saying about her was that she made everything better... She made everything better.

How on earth does one make everything better unless there is a more powerful source of love that surrounds them? These people are not mistakes; they were created so that the glory of God might be revealed in them. They still can serve a mighty purpose in the world. If only we began to see God's glory in a much bigger way; if we started to see God's glory in the seemingly lowly and mundane things of this world. Life is so precious, and it isn't something that should be "started over" simply because a child may be born differently than the rest of the world. Nor do I believe that we should shrink back in giving a child life because of the fear of suffering or what their lives might become, as Dawkins himself submits. Sure, it is absolutely gut-wrenching to see a child have to suffer due to the fact that they have a hundred or more seizures a day, but that still does indicate that that child is a joy and blessing to their families. Nor does it mean that the mad love of God is not sovereign overall life and can allow that child's life to be an instrument for His glory. Much more, maybe, God allows that child's life to exemplify His love to the parents or people taking care of the child.

Furthermore, a parent who is taking care of a child with Down Syndrome, epilepsy, or some sort of mental handicap, obviously isn't going to live forever. Thus it is a proper idea to set up a contingency plan, so that should something happen to them, their child will be taken care of. There are greater options than Dawkins suggests. Some doctors have told pregnant mothers whose children will have Down Syndrome that their child would be more like a fish than a human and only as smart as a baboon. It was always interesting to me how doctors could make such prophecies over a child's life, as though they can see down the spectrum of the child's life and see all that they will or will not become. This is exactly why I have come to trust less in man's professional opinion and to trust in God's sovereignty over everything that happens in life.

That isn't to say that all doctors don't know what they are talking about, or that we shouldn't trust them. The fact of the matter is that they are not the author and finisher of faith and life. I strongly believe that when we learn to see His glory in all of life, we are filled with deep bravery and the ability to trust in Him no matter what happens in our lives because we know that He is in control and is always out for our good, however hard it is to see, know, and understand at times. Life may seem darkest at certain times, but He is the light and hope that pulls us through any and all things. Though I am not a parent with a special needs child, I do know what it is like to interact with someone who is mentally handicapped. He heavily leans on the care of others, and I'm not sure that he can fully comprehend the full message of the Gospel.

But I do pray for him; I try to teach him right from wrong. I trust that God knows His condition. I've learned that sometimes the best thing we can do is pray and place the ones we love in the loving hands of God because that is the best and safest place that they can be. When I was a young boy in middle school, there was a special needs classroom on the lower level. I sometimes didn't like how sectioned off these special kids were. Looking back, I'm sure that a few of them had autism and Down Syndrome, while a few others I knew were severely mentally handicapped. Every week, I would get permission from my teacher to walk down to the classroom to help out. All the kids were awesome in their own way, but there were a few kids in particular who drew my attention. The first kid—his name was Ernie, and early on I could tell that he maybe had the mental capacity of a young child. He loved to read books about Bert and Ernie. He would always be so happy to see me, and he would come up to me and give me a hug. Some of the staff would have to watch when he hugged people because he liked to grab hair. I didn't know why at the time, but I loved Ernie and everyone in the classroom. It would shatter my heart every time he had a severe seizure, the kind that had put me in the hospital as a kid. Another person who caught my attention—we'll just call her Amy because I don't actually remember her name. But she too would light up when she saw me; she would point to me and make sure everyone in the classroom knew of my presence. She was a hugger, too, and I remember her trying to do math that was way below her age level, but she was always so happy. Again, I'm not sure that she could grasp larger concepts such as good, evil, injustice, and things of that nature. All she wanted to do was be happy and hug people. After I graduated junior high, I never saw any of these kids again.

God has always brought them back to my attention, though, and I often speculate as to whether or not they will be in the arms of God when they die. I believe so because I trust that He is good and that He will do what is right. I believe that the mad love of God automatically swallows them up into His presence, which is for His glory because He is good. In this way, you can fall deeply on God's love, grace, and mercy.

## Question for Reflection

Do you know anyone in your life with a developmental disability who can see the glory of God upon them? Moreover, as an image-bearer of God, do you see the immense value that your own life has?

# 29
# A Mad Love Legacy

"A new commandment I give to you, that you love one another: just as I have loved you, you also are to love one another. By this all people will know that you are my disciples, if you have love for one another."
John 13:34-35 (ESV)

WHAT WE DO IN LIFE echoes in eternity, as Maximus said to his troops as they were getting ready for battle. His words could not be more true, for, as followers of Christ, what we do in this life does echo in eternity. It is not a fruitful mindset to simply believe that knowing Christ is a simple exit strategy out of this life. Though the next stop for us after our earthly lives in eternity with Christ, I truly believe that He desires for us to leave the best legacy behind us that we can, by His grace alone. It may be tempting to think to yourself that you have made too much of a mess of your life to come anywhere close to leaving a legacy behind you. Maybe you think the only legacy that you have or can leave is the legacy of shame, regret, and mistakes.

I'm not going to lie to you, some people do in fact die in such a state. But I don't believe that has to be you. Not any longer. I have always believed that even on one's deathbed it is still possible to leave a lasting, changing memory behind. What I mean is that a person could have lived their life with a heart full of bitterness, resentment, and anger, and on their deathbed, they still can decide to forgive and let go of the past. Does this cancel everything else that has taken place in the span of life? It doesn't, but at the very best, those thoughts and feelings have been sent away. The mad love of God can take the person who feels like the biggest mess and failure and make them a person of hope and triumph. If we may visit the story of the prodigal son once again, I love that the English Standard Version (ESV) uses the word squandered. Verse 13 says,

"He squandered his property in reckless living." How does a person like this son go on making a legacy with his own life? Simple—it has nothing to do with his own merit or strength but is based on the fact that he is now caught up in a mad love legacy, the love that his father has for him. That truly is the greatest legacy that one could ever be brought into; why? Because the old truly becomes new. In John 3:3, Jesus says, "Truly, truly, I say to you, unless one is born again, he cannot see the kingdom of God" (ESV). Here, Jesus is speaking to Nicodemus, who was a man who strove to follow all the rules that God passed down through Moses. He was probably someone who lived a morally upright existence, someone who knew God's law inside and out and believed in his heart that that was enough. Enough to merit him eternal life by himself.

In other words, he is the equivalent of someone in today's society who says:

I don't do drugs

I don't steal

I give money or food to the poor

I put others before myself

(fill in the blank)

I'm a good person, God!

Much like Nicodemus, we can, in fact, be a good and morally upright person and still not have a heart that has been changed by the mad love of God. The truth is that when we are focused on our own moral perfection according to the letter of the law, we are not actually thinking about anybody else but ourselves and where our own righteousness can lead us. Being born again is likened to having the warm heat melt off the frost on the windows of a car. Or, quite possibly, a better way of looking at it is the way it is portrayed in the first movie in the Chronicles of Narnia. Aslan simply breathes on Mr. Tumnus who is frozen, and his frozen body returns to its normal state.

The point to notice is that as the ice is melting off his body, it is actually painful. Sin is like cancer to the soul, and the only way for it to be removed from our lives is if God becomes the ultimate surgeon and removes it for us. Scripture tells us that the word of God is like a two-edged sword:

"For the word of God is living and active, sharper than any two-edged sword, piercing to the division of soul and of spirit, of joints and of marrow, and discerning the thoughts and intentions of the heart" (Hebrews 4:12, ESV).

For Nicodemus, Jesus is cutting down to the very core of who he is. He is cutting away at all his religious piety, which Nicodemus thinks will save him and gain approval and the affection of God. He thinks that when he dies, he will be remembered for his zeal and morally rigorous lifestyle. To be clear, it's not that living with morals is wrong, it's that he is missing the mad love of God to go along with how he is already living. In the Gospel of Luke (Chapter 18), Jesus is confronted by a young man who is very wealthy, and their conversation unfolds like this:

"A certain ruler asked him, 'Good teacher, what must I do to inherit eternal life?'

'Why do you call me good?' Jesus answered. 'No one is good—except God alone. You know the commandments: "You shall not commit adultery, you shall not murder, you shall not steal, you shall not give false testimony, honor your father and mother."' 'All these I have kept since I was a boy,' he said. When Jesus heard this, he said to him, 'You still lack one thing. Sell everything you have and give to the poor, and you will have treasure in heaven. Then come, follow me.' When he heard this, he became very sad because he was very wealthy. Jesus looked at him and said, 'How hard it is for the rich to enter the kingdom of God! Indeed, it is easier for a camel to go through the eye of a needle than for someone who is rich to enter the kingdom of God'" (NIV).

Once again, we have someone who has a lot of head knowledge about what it means to be a good person on the surface, but his heart is not actually connecting to the embodiment of truth. When Jesus asks him, "Why do you call me good? Only God is good," I believe that Jesus is not questioning his own self-identification as much as He is getting at what this young man actually believes. Does he believe that Jesus is who He says He is? He alludes to not knowing because he calls Jesus "good teacher," which is no different than what some people think of Christ today. But here we see Jesus cutting and hacking away at his heart, and it's clear that he only wants eternal life for eternal life's sake, not the person who actually gives eternal life in the first place. This young man's heart is not transformed by the mad love of God. Rather, he is an addict unto himself who loves his possessions so much that the very thought of losing them causes him great inward sorrow. The person who has their heart touched by the mad love of God first understands that no amount of right living could ever purchase them eternal life. They understand that the price Christ paid for our purchase is far greater than anything they could ever amount to. Secondly, they understand that when they encounter this love, it humbles them in a way that offers them the truest reflection of their own depravity. Yet they are always filled with a love that frees them from shame and self-loathing. And thirdly, the mad love of God frees them to give not only earthly possessions but also to give love away freely.

The mad love legacy starts from having a changed heart, and it comes with a sober and grateful understanding of who we are in Christ. It makes us brave to share His love with others freely. This is a part of myself and my faith that I have been slowly trying to rekindle. I used to be fearless to share my faith; I didn't care if someone thought I was stupid because I believed that Christ died on the cross for my sins; I didn't care if someone thought I was crazy to actually believe that God created the world. Somewhere along the way, something happened to me. It has grieved my heart ever since.

Somehow, I was duped into thinking that I could hide the light of Christ because that's what the enemy wants. He whispers for us to be silent, telling us, "It's okay; don't say things that disturb a person's foundation." Except, that's not what Christ did. He made all kinds of people mad, He offended a lot of people, He flipped people on their heads (spiritually speaking), and He changed the very essence of a person's life and existence with deep ferocity and love. And what we do as Christians with the love that God has graciously and madly given us means everything. The mad love legacy allows us to listen and understand the stories of people that we encounter on a daily basis without having a sense of inner superiority. For example, in John 8, we see the story of a woman caught in adultery. The religious leaders (scribes and Pharisees) bring a woman to Jesus, who, for lack of better words, has slept around. In that context, the wages for adultery were to be stoned to death. These religious leaders were more than likely looking down on this woman. I dare not imagine what they must have said to her when they found her or how they treated her as they brought her to Jesus.

I can, however, imagine the shame and regret that she was feeling in her own heart. And Jesus knew that as He looked into the woman's eyes. He could see the smug and pious looks, not only on their faces but also in their hearts. Jesus bent down and began to write in the sand with His finger. What did He write? No one truly knows; some have speculated that He bent down and wrote the sins of the religious leaders in the sand, which I would agree with, as well. In their hearts, they knew what the answer was for someone like this woman, but they only went to Jesus to see what He would say.

They wanted Jesus to say, "Take her away and stone her!" but His response again cuts away at what they believe. He says to them, "Let

## A Mad Love Legacy

him who is without sin among you be the first to throw a stone at her." I can only imagine the looks on their faces as they heard the stern words of Jesus; His words were like a heavy sledgehammer to their souls. One by one, I can imagine the religious leaders throwing down their stones and walking away with the same sorrow the rich young ruler had experienced. Jesus knew that the wages of sin is and was death. The difference was that He did not look down on this woman the same way the religious leaders did. Instead, He looked upon her with grace and the mad love of God. If I had been this woman, I would have been utterly astounded and shocked. She was probably thinking to herself, "What!? You don't condemn me?"

For she knew and expected that what awaited her was her death and rightly expected and thought that Jesus would be angry with her and send her away. I can imagine Jesus squatting down to be eye level with her, and she probably had a sense of holy terror inside her, as he gently and firmly commanded her to go and sin no more. I truly believe that to live out the mad love legacy, loving each other and others in this way is key. And as Paul reminds us in 1 Corinthians 6:11:

"And such were some of you. But you were washed, you were sanctified, you were justified in the name of the Lord Jesus Christ and by the Spirit of our God" (ESV). We were once like this woman, deserving death for our sins, swallowed up by shame and regret, unsure that there was a way to start over again and be at peace with the past. But the mad love of God washed us from our sin, it sanctified us (set us apart), and we were justified because of what Christ did on our behalf. Justification in simple terms is being declared not guilty in the sight of God. When we truly know and understand this truth, we no longer can look down on someone who is living apart from the mad love of God because we have lived that way, too.

The difference now, after knowing this sobering reality, is that we can offer the greatest hope. The hope that the Father offers us, through

A Mad Love & A Shameless Audacity

His beloved Son Jesus Christ. When listening and responding, compassion and empathy are vital elements. In life and even in sharing our faith, we are so quick to respond rather than listening to understand. In Mark 9, a father brings his son who has been having seizures; obviously, Jesus already knew everything about the young boy, and He already knew about the father's immense distress. Jesus asks the boy's father, "How long has he been like this?" Again, Jesus is all-knowing from the start. I believe that He is actually displaying empathy, love, and compassion for the grief of the father and the suffering of his son. More than that, after He enters in with empathy, love, and compassion, He then moves to the truth. He moves to the stance of the man's heart. The young boy's father has a hard time believing that Jesus can actually heal his son. After all, his son has had this condition since birth, and his father probably has taken him down various avenues for a cure.

In Verse 22, the boy's father says to Jesus, "If you can do anything, take pity on us." Jesus engages with this man's heart, confronting the reality of his doubt and what he thought was possible. The boy's father exclaims with almost a cry in his voice, "I do believe, help me overcome my unbelief!" Once again, we are left not knowing what becomes of the young boy and his father. But it would be easy to speculate that this man had his life utterly changed by the love-filled truth that Jesus had shown him. Dare I say that from this point on, he probably lived a legacy believing the truth of who Christ was and living in the realm of possibility, as well as rearing his son in this way? This is exactly what happens when we share the mad love of God with others. The possibility of life-altering change becomes real. Consider the words of Isaiah 61:1-4 (ESV):

"The Spirit of the Lord GOD is upon me,
because the LORD has anointed me
to bring good news to the poor;
he has sent me to bind up the brokenhearted,
to proclaim liberty to the captives,

and the opening of the prison to those who are bound

to proclaim the year of the LORD's favor,

and the day of vengeance of our God;

to comfort all who mourn;

to grant to those who mourn in Zion—

to give them a beautiful headdress instead of ashes,

the oil of gladness instead of mourning,

the garment of praise instead of a faint spirit;

that they may be called oaks of righteousness,

the planting of the LORD, that he may be glorified.

They shall build up the ancient ruins;

they shall raise up the former devastations;

they shall repair the ruined cities,

the devastations of many generations."

Though this is a proclamation of the coming Messiah Jesus and all that He would do, I believe that when we have His Spirit inside us, our mission becomes very similar. He works through us and in us to bring hope to the hopeless, the poor in spirit, and those who are prisoners in themselves. This, in many ways, is our life's greatest purpose first and foremost; everything else falls under that purpose. Oh, but how often do I (we) forget such a reality? How much more time is burned up in our lives seeking our life's calling and vocation than sharing the good news?

The hesitation comes in when we begin to feel that we don't have a good enough message, meaning that you don't believe you have a very compelling or eloquent testimony. I have struggled with this belief for the longest time, for the simple reason that I'm not the best in the areas of apologetics, science, and philosophy. Though those close to me assure me that I am very sharp, I often feel dumb or stupid and often keep silent. One thing that I have had to truly burn into my being, though, is: It isn't me or you who convinces or converts anyone to Christ; it is all about the work of the Holy Spirit. Consider the words of John 14:26, "But the Advocate, the Holy Spirit, whom the Father will send in my name, will teach you all things and will remind you of everything I have said to you" (NIV). Or Mark 13:11, which reads, "Whenever you are arrested and brought to trial, do not worry beforehand about what to say. Just say whatever is given you at the time, for it is not you speaking, but the Holy Spirit" (NIV).

We have to remember, then, to be completely reliant and dependent upon Him in prayer. Once again, this is not something I am the best at, and often I rely on my own knowledge and wisdom, which ends up failing more than anything. How much braver and galvanized would we be in proclaiming our faith to others if this were the case? Probably much more so; the mad love legacy is dependent upon our love for others and the Holy Spirit at the same time. The love that the Father has lavished upon us (1 John 3:1) should make our hearts ache and shatter for those who do not know of His mad love. And if that's the case, that means that it's on us to pray, love, and go forth, as we feel the Spirit is leading us to share.

Furthermore, consider the words of the Apostle Paul on the matter in 1 Corinthians 2:1-5:

"And I, when I came to you brothers, did not come proclaiming to you the testimony of God with lofty speech or wisdom. For I decided to know nothing among you except Jesus Christ and him crucified. And I was with you in weakness and in fear and in much trembling, and my speech and my message were not in plausible words of wisdom, but in demonstration of the spirit and of power, so that your faith might not rest on the wisdom of men but in the power of God" (ESV).

In other words, he is saying that he came with a very raw and basic message, but one that was wrapped in love and truth. He, Paul, doesn't present an argument that is layered in apologetics, science, or philosophy. Instead, he says that his message is the message of Christ and Him

A Mad Love Legacy

crucified, which in the end is all that we Christians need to present as the good news to those we encounter. This is the only real message that I have as well.

1) God loves you and sent His only Son to die for you.

2) You need to repent and trust in God.

3) And, should you not, you will spend eternity in Hell.

It's pretty straightforward, I know, and some might even label it as intolerant and narrow-minded, but there actually is more that can and should be added under each area we use to share our faith. Obviously, the sharing of the good news of God should not be reduced to a mere formula. It should always be a fresh and organic experience, meaning that with each person with whom you share the good news, it should be as though you are listening and responding to their story and questions as if it were the first time (as R.C. Sproul once wonderfully said).

Sharing the good news of the Gospel and the mad love of God should not be something that we drag around with us because we have to do it. It should be done out of deep desire because we want to do it. I truly worry about followers of Christ and myself who sometimes feel that the sharing of our faith is done out of dreadful submission or obedience because we should never lose sight of how madly the Father has loved us in His Son Jesus and the price that was paid for us.

Consider this deep love once again through the words of John 15:9:

"As the father has loved me, so have I loved you" (ESV). It's such a small sentence, but it is loaded with such a fierce and mad love. And only when I was reading it aloud with my girlfriend did I realize the depth of its power. Showing this love in a much more deep way, let us look at John 17:23-25:

"I in them and you in me, that they may become perfectly one, so that the world may know that you sent me and loved them even as you loved me. Father, I desire that they also, whom you have given me, may be with me where I am, to see my glory that you have given me because you loved me before the foundation of the world. O righteous Father, even though the world does not know you, I know you, and these know that you have sent me" (ESV).

Take a moment and see the weight of what is going on in this passage, and once you truly see I have no doubt that it will utterly blow your mind and change your life, as it has mine. This passage is a glorious example and display of the love that flows between and throughout the Father and Son and the Trinity in general. First, Jesus prays that the body of Christ become one, just as the Father and Son are one in unison. Secondly, Jesus prays that His followers may be with Christ and share in the same glory that the Father magnifies the Son with and vice versa. And thirdly, this love that that exists between the Father and Son is the same love that existed in Genesis 1 where it reads, "Let us make man in our own image."

This love existed before the very foundation of the world and was graciously and beautifully given through the creation of the world and the rescue mission that Jesus Christ was sent on into this world, to draw broken people like myself unto Himself. Furthermore, Christ loves those He draws to Himself so madly and deeply that He takes upon Himself our sin, shame, and regret, and gives us His love, righteousness, grace, and holiness, which makes the Father see us (his beloved children) as perfect, perfect in His sight. This, my friends, is the exact same love and amazing grace that we get to share with those around us with great love and joy, not because we have to, but because we want to and because He has called us friends (John 15:15). We become friends with not only the risen Christ, but His Father looks upon us with delight and mad love as well. We all get to share in His grace and mad love, with the power of the Holy Spirit. But I also believe that we can do so with spiritual authority. In Luke 10:18-20, Jesus says this in regard to spiritual authority:

"And he said to them, 'I saw Satan fall like lightning from heaven. Behold, I have given you authority to tread on serpents and scorpions, and overall the power of the enemy, and nothing shall hurt you. Nevertheless, do not rejoice in this, that the spirits are subject to you, but rejoice that your names are written in heaven'" (ESV).

Jesus is telling this to His disciples, but I truly believe that you and I can have the ability to exercise the same spiritual authority in our lives and the world today. When we believe that the Father has loved us so deeply and madly in Christ, we furthermore have the ability and spiritual authority first to silence and trample on the enemy (again) in our own lives and in the lives of others. Now, I would argue that the concept of spiritual warfare and authority can tend to weird people out. We think of people praying in tongues, being slain in the Spirit, healing, and casting demons out in Jesus' name, which can be and is a part of spiritual authority and warfare, but I don't believe that it always has to be filled with dramatic or over-emotional experience. Rather, it is knowing the power that we have in Jesus' name.

Power in Jesus' name… This means that (in quite simple terms) when I am experiencing shameful and condemning thoughts that are not of God, I have the authority to tell these thoughts and the founder of these thoughts to shut up in Jesus' name. I can say that to my own anxiety and depression as well. I in no way intend to make spiritual authority out to be some sort of magic pill because sometimes when I try to exercise that same authority in my own life, things don't merely disappear all at once. But I know who truly has all authority over all of my life. Spiritual authority is also opening up Scripture every single day, reflecting on it, and even memorizing it. Scripture memorization is a crucial practice because when it comes to our own lives, it allows us to have Scripture handy that we can call upon when the time comes. For His Word has the power to move and change us from the inside out.

2 Timothy 3:16-17 says, "All Scripture is God-breathed and is useful for teaching, rebuking, correcting and training in righteousness, so that the servant of God may be thoroughly equipped for every good work" (NIV). All Scripture is God-breathed, meaning that all Scripture has God's authority infused into it and thus has the ability to move in and change our mental, emotional, and spiritual outlook on our lives. When we know the spiritual authority we can exercise in our own lives and who the authority actually comes from, we then have that same authority to go out and speak into the lives of others. When we speak of the mad love legacy, it should not only exemplify love and grace, but it should also be filled with authority and truth. A truth that we can both claim and stand on, especially, as it relates to living a life based on prayer. As it relates to my own mad love legacy, I know it won't be based on the fact that I am a gifted evangelist, but I most certainly want it to reflect a life of prayer. I love that in Acts 2:42, not only did they devote themselves to the apostle's teaching and the breaking of bread, but also to prayer. Some years ago, when I was attending my first Bible school, we were doing a youth rally at a high school. After we had finished setting up, we gathered for pizza.

Before we ate, the pastor who was going to lead the rally with his message made it clear that on this night, people would have different roles to serve in. He especially highlighted that some people's role would simply be to pray. As he said that, he looked at me with a smile on his face. That night, the rally didn't bring as big a turnout as we had hoped (not that it's all about the numbers). One of the directors spoke up when we reconvened after the rally. She simply said, "Guys, imagine how much more impact we could have had if we had all prayed more." I truly believe that God (in love) used her words to cut into our hearts, to make us understand that everything in life is dependent on prayer. Even though God is wholly sovereign over all things in life and doesn't need us to pray, the fact is that He longs for and wants us to pray. I even believe that He loves the voices of His beloved children.

Entertaining a thought, though, what if your only life's purpose and mission in life were to pray? Would you be okay with that? What if you could not physically speak but instead could write and pray, would that be enough for you? Better yet, would HE be enough for you? How we answer this is so important to our spiritual vitality. Too often, I believe we allow ourselves to get wrapped up in all the wrong things. Let us fixate on the words in 2 Timothy 2:3-5:

"Share in suffering as a good soldier of Christ Jesus. No soldier gets entangled in civilian pursuits since his aim is to please the one who enlisted him. An athlete is not crowned unless he competes according to the rules" (ESV).

In life, I believe that we allow our legacy to reflect our education, accomplishments, and even our bank accounts. And, while none of that is bad, in the grand scheme of eternity all of these things are temporary and are not of any value to our spiritual legacy and what our truest focus was in life. Was it man's approval, worldly affection, and praise, or was it the One who graciously enlisted us into His kingdom? It's amazing to me how all we hold so dear and what we think is important can be taken from us at a moment's notice. In these moments, we begin to realize what truly matters, and it's not external. As Christians and as beloved children of God, we have the truest understanding of this reality, in that the external focus is fleeting, and God's love for us puts everything in a much clearer perspective for us.

I've always had a profound respect for those who have suffered real persecution and even died for the faith and love that they have for Jesus Christ. There is a Christian pastor who has been a pastor in Turkey for twenty-three years, and since October 2016 he has been detained on charges of espionage and apparent links to a terror organization. The pastor firmly denies the allegations, and others have speculated that there is some political issue in the matter. During the first several months of his sentence, it was said that he lost up to fifty pounds and suffered from severe depression. I was reading up on the pastor's life, and I discovered that he had a house church of twenty-five people. I tend to think about how God is allowing this man to teach the Scriptures to God's people and how God might be using this man to communicate His love to this small number of people and, furthermore, to get them ready for His kingdom. In our American churches, we tend to focus on church growth, bringing more people into our sanctuaries. And sometimes this is done with more attractions, i.e. big screens, big hype and show in our times of worship, and even our own coffee shops. Now, if all this brings people to know the mad love of God for the first time, great. But do we actually need these other elements that are just fluff at the end of the day? I would say an emphatic no because if the message of the Gospel is not enough on its own for us to communicate grace, love, and truth, then we have a real problem on our hands.

Imagine being this pastor for a moment, having a group of people in his home each Sunday and probably frequent visitors each week. I'd imagine that he had a small home with just enough to live off each week, yet by the grace of God he still tries to be hospitable by offering food, water, and etc. He doesn't have the attraction of a nice church with comfortable seating and huge screens with a band playing hypnotic worship songs. All he probably has is the Holy Spirit and the Scriptures in hand, and the community has their voices that they can raise up to offer their praise and adoration to God. That is more than enough, and dare I say all that you need? And now this pastor has endured the harsh conditions of prison for charges that are a blanket covering for the reality that he is a Christian.

I don't know much at all about the state of his soul right now, other than that he has endured great depression. But I have to believe that the Holy Spirit was and is his all-sustaining power and that the mad love of God strengthened him not to shrink back in his faith but to even share it with the other prisoners near him (this is all speculation). I love the story of the Apostle Paul and Silas in Acts 16. Paul and Silas are captured, beaten, and thrown into prison after Paul commands an evil spirit to come out of a girl who was held as a slave by her captors. This girl was apparently good at fortune-telling and made her captors a good deal of money. In Verse 18, it says that Paul became "greatly annoyed." Now, from the human side of things, I find that phrase to be somewhat comforting, as I cannot be alone in being greatly annoyed at times. I doubt that Paul was annoyed with the girl herself, but more so with the evil spirit inside her. He then executed the spiritual authority that had been granted to him by the Holy Spirit and said, "I command you in the name of Jesus Christ to come out of her."

When the girl's captors saw the authority which Paul and Silas had inside them and that these men were a significant threat to their greedy hearts, they had them captured and beaten, saying that they were disrupting the peace and teaching customs that were not acceptable by Roman standards. In reality, though, they were deeply threatened by the Christ who lived inside of both Paul and Silas. The real joy of the passage comes as they were both sitting in prison. I picture it as a dark and gloomy setting; they were both singing hymns to the glory of God, and all the other prisoners could hear their voices. I wonder if they were all moved by it as well. The passage then tells us that suddenly there was a massive earthquake, and the prison doors shot open. The guard who was on post to watch them awoke, and he quickly drew his sword and was going to kill himself because the fact that he had allowed them to escape would have brought a great deal of shame upon him.

Paul cried out, "Do not harm yourself; we are all here!" The jailor then demanded that the lights be lit, and he rushed in and asked, "Sirs, what must I do to be saved?" Paul and Silas both responded with a very simple and direct message: believe in the Lord Jesus, and you will be saved, you and your household. The rest of the section goes like this:

"Then they spoke the word of the Lord to him and to all the others in his house. At that hour of the night the jailer took them and washed their wounds; then immediately he and all his household were baptized. The jailer brought them into his house and set a meal before them; he was filled with joy because he had come to believe in God—he and his whole household" (Acts 16:32-34, NIV).

Paul, much like the pastor mentioned above, was persecuted for his faith and belief in the mad love of God. What excites me and saddens me in the same breath, is the boldness and courage that Paul and Silas were armed with. Even in spite of all the suffering that Paul endured, he still managed to retain his joy and offer up his voice with Silas while in prison.

In my own life, it saddens me because you and I may never face the persecution that the pastor, the Apostle Paul, or any other Christian in another country may face on a daily basis. And yet, I fear people ridiculing me for my beliefs and the probability of them calling me stupid or anything that falls into that category. In all truth, the mad love legacy requires us to have a shameless audacity in our faith in the risen Jesus and to not keep silent about the cause of the good news and how it has changed our lives. Even though I truly believe that Jesus Christ still loved Peter madly after he denied Him three times, that should not be the disposition of our own hearts, though I submit out of the honesty of my own soul that maybe I have denied Christ in the quiet parts of myself, when I probably should have said something but didn't. Nor have I always lived in ways that honor and bring glory to His name, but I still have the shameless audacity to come before Him for forgiveness and grace because I know He loves me madly. In the Gospel of Matthew (10:32-33) Jesus says:

"So everyone who acknowledges me before men, I also will acknowledge before my Father who is in heaven, but whoever denies me before men, I also will deny before my Father who is in heaven" (ESV).

To be completely honest, this passage and similar passages like this have always freaked me out because I have held back in the name of fear and not spoken of the name of Christ, and I can only imagine how much that has grieved the heart of God. Do I believe in the mad love that God has for me? Sometimes I do because I know that if I were God, I'd boot myself out of God's love and kingdom all at once. Yet, with those thoughts, I have to believe that the mad love of God is not based on my own thoughts, mood, or disposition. Or, as Brennan Manning wrote in his memoir All is Grace:

"Do you believe that the God of Jesus loves you beyond worthiness and unworthiness, beyond fidelity and infidelity—that he loves you in the morning sun and in the evening rain—that he loves you when your intellect denies it, your emotions refuse it, your whole being rejects it? Do you believe that God loves without condition or reservation and loves you this moment as you are and not as you should be?"

Do we know and trust that God loves us in this way? Do we trust that He loves, adores, and delights in us even on our most shameful, regretful, and darkest day? Do we know that even on our best days, even our greatest works cannot make Him love us more, based on our own effort and merit? Do we know that His love for us is always constant? Let the words of Psalm 117:2 truly sink into our very beings:

"For great is his steadfast love toward us, and the faithfulness of the LORD endures forever. Praise the LORD!" (ESV)

When we know how deep and wide the love of Christ is and believe that nothing can remove us from the love of God (Romans 8:31-39) and that when we are truly born again by the Holy Spirit we are sealed by the Holy Spirit (Ephesians 1), we can repent before God of our cowardice with a shameless audacity, knowing that He loves us so much. We can then boldly rise and allow the Holy Spirit to fill us with the confidence we need to speak of Jesus' name. Once again, consider the reality that Peter denied Christ publicly three times, even when he said that he would never deny Jesus. And yet, in Acts 4:8-12 Peter is filled with such boldness and in 4:23-31:

"When they were released, they went to their friends and reported what the chief priests and the elders had said to them. And when they heard it, they lifted their voices together to God and said, 'Sovereign Lord, who made the heaven and the earth and the sea and everything in them, who through the mouth of our father David, your servant, said by the Holy Spirit,

"Why did the Gentiles rage, and the people plot in vain? The kings of the earth set themselves, and the rulers were gathered together, against the Lord and against his Anointed"—for truly in this city there were gathered together against your holy servant Jesus, whom you anointed, both Herod and Pontius Pilate, along with the Gentiles and the peoples of Israel, to do whatever your hand and your plan had predestined to take place. And now, Lord, look upon their threats and grant to your servants to continue to speak your word with all boldness, while you stretch out your hand to heal, and signs and wonders are performed through the name of your holy servant Jesus.' And when they had prayed, the place in which they were gathered together was shaken, and they were all filled with the Holy Spirit and continued to speak the word of God with boldness" (ESV).

One of the greatest signs, in my opinion, that Christ is real is the way His message changes lives. The Apostle Paul is, once again, a prime example, one who persecuted Christians and was behind the murder of Stephen. And yet, when we arrive at Acts 16, the apostle is quite literally knocked on his rump. He has a life-changing encounter with the risen Christ, and he goes from being a persecutor and murderer of Christians to one who has his life changed from the inside out because of the mad love of God. People are even skeptical of his changed life; it takes time for people to believe him and that he has truly met the risen Jesus. Once again, Peter went from being a coward and numbskull to being a brave and bold witness for the mad love of God. He wasn't afraid to proclaim and stand up to the Roman authorities. If we, too, have had our lives changed by the mad love of God, then it is now our joy and duty to do something with that which has changed our lives.

As the flame of our lives burns out, we can leave behind us echoes of the mad love of God with our words and deeds. As Christ-followers, that should be the main purpose and mission of our lives, and everything else should be secondary. The mission that God sends us out on is twofold:

1) We are to be mindful that we all love the Lord with all our heart, soul, mind, and strength and to love our neighbors always.

2) We are, then, commanded to go out and make disciples, baptizing them in the name of the Father, Son, and Holy Spirit.

It's pretty straightforward, but yet very difficult at the same time. Difficult because, on one hand, it demands that we be both mindful and watchful of our own hearts by asking ourselves the simple question, "Am I loving the Lord with all of me? Am I truly loving my neighbor as myself?" It's good to ask ourselves and take stock of whether or not we are truly allowing the mad love of God to consume all of our being, or if we simply have a mental understanding of His love. If we are not cognizant of the reality of loving Him with all our being, there then is a very big chance that we are not allowing the Spirit to draw us into a deeper understanding and dependency. Thus, we can find ourselves loving from our own will and strength, which can be deadly, as it relates to loving our neighbors. When we love out of our own strength, we aren't loving them from and out of the mad love of God. But when we are loving God with all our being, heart, and mind, we then do so with a far greater scope of eternity and genuine understanding of how God has changed our lives. In other words, I am saying that it is possible to truly know and understand God's mad love for us, and it's truly possible to convey that love in a genuine way so that people know we actually believe this, rather than just feeding them spiritualized hype. We can truly know that God loves us, even when we don't feel worthy and lovable. Even when I am deep in my own despair and sadness, I still know and trust that He loves me madly, for nothing is more freeing and liberating in every possible way, shape, and form. I love the words in Hebrews 13:8:

"Jesus Christ is the same yesterday and today and forever" (NIV).

Jesus Christ does not change. His character does not change, and therefore, His love for you does not change. If that is true, we can walk through life with great confidence and boldness. I know that I am exhausting the subject, but it's only because I am so deeply passionate and confident that Christians and people, in general, lack a profound understanding of the love of God, and as such, we are not experiencing life and love to the fullest. I truly believe that the mad love of God can and does change the way we live. And if it isn't changing how and what we believe, then something is off in our walk with God. If the mad love of God has changed our lives, then a suitable response must follow. I think Romans 6:1-6 is the best response:

"What shall we say then? Are we to continue in sin that grace may abound? By no means! How can we who died to sin still live in it? Do you not know that all of us who have been baptized into Christ Jesus were baptized into his death? We were buried therefore with him by baptism into death, in order that, just as Christ was raised from the dead by the glory of the Father, we too might walk in newness of life. For if we have been united with him in a death like his, we shall certainly be united with him in a resurrection like his. We know that our old self was crucified with him in order that the body of sin might be brought to nothing so that we would no longer be enslaved to sin" (ESV).

If the mad love of God has truly overcome the condition of our hearts, then we must make every effort, by His grace, to no longer let sin reign in our minds and hearts. Just because one cannot exhaust the grace of God, it is by no means a free pass to live recklessly. We must allow the Spirit to put our sin under His submission because of His great and mad love for us. Living a life that is counterproductive to the grace of God, that is, willfully sinning and living in destructive ways, is an abuse of the grace of God and a grave sign of a lack of understanding of the great sacrifice that Christ offered for you in His death, burial, and resurrection.

We have died a spiritual death with Christ; that means our sinful nature was put to death with Christ. But we were raised into the newness of life as Paul says in Verse 4. This means, once again, that we are spotless, holy, and blameless in the King's eyes. This means that we are new creations in Christ Jesus. This means that we are no longer enslaved to sin, spiritual bondage, and even mental and emotional bondage. And, when we truly know and understand this, our mad love legacy truly begins. Our mission and purpose are to make much of Him and to be satisfied in Him. As John Piper says: God is most glorified in us when we are most satisfied in Him. We bring glory to His name by being satisfied in Him. Being satisfied with Him is crucial. We are most satisfied in Him when we are most cognizant of what He has done for us and who we are in Him. When we are satisfied with Him, we can joyfully and gladly focus on the mission ahead. What is the mission? Making disciples. Jesus says in Mathew 28:19-20:

"Go therefore and make disciples of all nations, baptizing them in[a] the name of the Father and of the Son and of the Holy Spirit, teaching them to observe all that I have commanded you. And behold, I am with you always, to the end of the age" (ESV).

This, in simple terms, means: sharing the good news with others, not being afraid to open your mouth. In the Gospel of Mark (Chapter 5), there is a man who had been under extreme torment by demons, to the extent that that people were afraid to go near him, and rightfully so. But Jesus casts the demons out from the mind of this man and clothes him in white, which is a symbol of purity. I love the phrase "in his right mind." This man was so radically changed by his encounter with Jesus that he wanted to go with Jesus wherever He went. Yet Jesus simply told him to go and tell others about what God had done for him. As it reads in Verses 19-20:

"Go home to your friends and tell them how much the Lord has done for you, and how he had mercy on you. And he went away and began to proclaim in the Decapolis how much Jesus had done for him, and everyone marveled" (ESV).

How simple a command and how simple a mission, and yet we as Christians make it all the more complicated. I would imagine that the man only had the story of who he once was and how Jesus Christ had changed his life. And that truly is all you need, that and a heart of compassion, empathy, and a listening ear. The passage tells us that everyone marveled at the man's inner and outer transformation. Inasmuch as everyone marveled, does that then mean that they were changed in the same way this man was? No one can be truly sure, but as Paul mentions in 1 Corinthians 3:6:

"I planted, Apollos watered, but God gave the growth" (ESV). Here, Paul mentions a trifecta, but in all, it is God who gave and provided the growth. So it is in our daily interactions with people, especially when it comes to faith. Perhaps you are the one who simply plants a seed in the being of another person, and you prayerfully move on. Then, someone else comes along and helps provide that seed with water, but it is the Holy Spirit who actually causes life and growth. I believe that, so many times, our focus is winning arguments, showing how much we know as opposed to actually speaking to the mind and soul of a person about God's mad love for them. Again, we must focus on the simple truths about what it means to believe in the Lord Jesus Christ. I can remember some years ago leading a Bible study/small group in my basement. I had a spot in my heart for those in the punk rock culture and still do. I felt that they were ostracized from the church (body of Christ), largely due to their outward appearance. So, I thought, if the church didn't want these kids, I would bring the Gospel and the message of God's love to them. In my group were kids who loved dressing in all black and listening to industrial types of metal and so on; some had grown up in church and had a beautiful response to Jesus. They just felt utterly misunderstood by a lot of people. They brought their friends, too. Some were even self-proclaimed agnostics or atheists, and some professed to be involved with witchcraft, which didn't strike fear in me at all. I kept my message simple: God loves you! He can make you a new person, and your past doesn't have to haunt you if you come to Him humbly and ask Him to forgive you and make you a new creation. In response to His love and forgiveness, it is up to you to now go tell others about it.

These kids kept coming week after week. Some wandered off because I guess they couldn't handle it or didn't want anything to do with it. But there was one girl (we shall call her "M"), a quiet soul, who kept showing up. She believed that all religions said the same thing and were equally full of cow dung. Yet, the more I and other members of the group kept pounding away, telling her that God's love is nothing like all the other world religions and that He was better than anything else that could possibly provide her with a momentary joy, the more her heart began to soften before our very eyes. Eventually, she allowed us to pray for her, and, at that moment, I believe that she encountered the mad love of God.

This should be what it's all about, being changed by the mad love of God from the inside out and then going out and simply reporting to others about what God has done with us and for us, keeping our mission and message as clear as possible. If we look back on when Paul and Silas were in prison, and we look at the simplicity of their message, it is wrapped in love and truth. In love, he speaks to the prison guard who is about to end his own life and wants to know how to be saved. Paul simply says, "Believe in the Lord Jesus, and you will be saved." We take that truth, and we willingly go out into the world to share this truth with others. Yet we must always be on guard because the enemy will whisper lies in our ears, even though we want to share this truth.

The enemy will tell you you're not good enough to share this message, you're too much of a mess, you don't actually believe this, and no one will listen to what you have to say. Yet we fight against and silence these lies by renewing our minds with the truth and having the shameless audacity to do it anyway! When the lies enter our minds and the condemnation sits heavy, and the enemy reminds us of how much we've blown it, the greatest weapon that we have is this one: Admit that we have blown it in many ways but that God's mad love and grace is far greater and bigger than all our sins and shortcomings.

Once again, Peter was probably one of the greatest screw-ups in the Bible, and yet he bravely proclaimed the message of the Gospel in Acts. The same with the Apostle Paul: he didn't wait until he got his life together or got a theology degree before he went out and began speaking about how Christ had changed his life. It's as though he instantly went out and started shamelessly proclaiming what Christ had done for him. I believe that that's the trap the enemy wants us to fall into—that we have to wait to be perfect or ready to share in the mad love of God. I don't believe that there will ever be a time when we are actually ready or that we will ever know enough to be ready.

I'm not saying that becoming more prepared or equipped is not of value; it is. Yet, I believe that more important is our dependency on the Spirit, in prayer, relying on Him to guide our speech, and the ability to communicate His mad love and grace in a clear way. By all means, and by His grace alone, work on living in step with His Spirit, to live a life of holiness and consistency, but the idea that we have to wait until we have our poop in a group before sharing the mad love of Christ is a fallacy from the mouth of the enemy.

In my estimation, I don't care if you've been a Christian for a week, a few months, or your entire life. If you truly have been changed by the mad love of God, it should be a personal joy to go out and freely share it with others. It is also equally important (secondly) to know the Scriptures as best we can, both for our own personal warfare and to respond when someone makes a false claim about God and the Scriptures. I cannot tell you the number of times that I quote Romans 8:1-2 to myself when the enemy attacks or that I remind myself of the love that God has lavished upon me in Ephesians 1. When I was in college, we had to memorize four passages of our choosing. While I don't remember the verses that I chose, I do remember being unsure that I could complete the task. I've never been the greatest at memorizing things that way. But it had to be done to pass the class, and I had to recite in front of the instructor, which freaked me out! I bravely set out to accomplish the task, saying the verse out loud and trying to repeat the passage by closing my eyes. More often than not, I missed a few words each time, but the more times I tried, the better I got at repeating the verses. I would practice reciting the passage to my classmate next to me, and even then, I screwed up. But, the moral of the story is, I got the job done. It is very possible, then, to get good at memorizing Scripture passages. Even if it's only small bits, if that's what you can do, then that's what you can do. Sure, it is always good to strive to memorize a bit more with time. But I also think that it is okay to do what you can.

It's also very important to be mindful of our beings as it relates to the enemy. I have noticed in my own life and heart that the enemy creeps in by whispering to me that I'm not a good Christian because I'm not like the Christians who can memorize entire books of the Bible or can pray for three or four hours each morning before even reading their Bibles! I do not believe that members of the body should ever feel shame or condemnation for what they can memorize or how much time they devote to prayer or other spiritual practices. Rather, a Christian should be looked upon for their own zeal for Christ, which looks different for each person. I don't think that God truly cares if you spend ten minutes in the Scriptures or three hours; He cares that you make time for Him and you put Him first. If you can spend longer periods of time in Scripture and in prayer each day, great. But I don't think how much time is spent in spiritual and faith practices every day should be the overall measuring stick. I think it is also important to know what the Bible says as it relates to combating lies and misconceptions that others may espouse. John Calvin writes, "A dog barks when his master is attacked. I would be a coward if I saw that God's truth is attacked and yet would remain silent." I agree with Calvin, and I am greatly convicted by his quote. How many times have I heard someone attack the word of God or God's character and said nothing but acted like a coward? Probably more times than I care to admit. The dog barks because the dog has a love for its master. I have a love for my Master as well, so why not respond when He is attacked? Truthfully speaking, I am not one who believes that God needs us to defend Him, but as His beloved, it should be our honor and joy to take up the cause of Christ and the mad ways that He has loved us.

I love the words that Paul writes in Acts 17:24-25:

"The God who made the world and everything in it, being Lord of heaven and earth, does not live in temples made by man, nor is he served by human hands, as though he needed anything, since he himself gives to all mankind life and breath and everything" (ESV). I believe that Paul emphasizes my point by saying that God is not served by human hands, for HE is the one who gives life and has existed before everything in existence. Rather, even though He needs nothing because He is sufficient in and of Himself, He shares the triune love with us as His people and thus gives us the joy, mission, and purpose of serving alongside Him in His ultimate mission.

## Question for Reflection

Let us ask ourselves a final sobering question: Examining our lives, do you feel that yours would speak to a legacy? Even on our death beds, we can leave a legacy behind just by doing the right thing and getting our hearts in order. But don't wait for the last breath of your life, start walking that path with the next breath – right now.

www.ingramcontent.com/pod-product-compliance
Lightning Source LLC
Chambersburg PA
CBHW050317120526
44592CB00014B/1939